Advance Praise for *Breathe Believe Balance*

'If you are looking for an "out-of-the-box" approach to performance enhancement, look no further. Shayamal Vallabhjee travelled with me on the ATP tour for six years, which includes two Olympic games. Much of the learnings in this book have helped me professionally and personally. Using science, Vallabhjee guides you to mould habits that will help you become the person you want to be'

Mahesh Bhupathi, 12 x Tennis Grand Slam Champion

'Based on expertise and experience gained from years of practice, both professional and spiritual, Shayamal has strung his pearls of wisdom together in *Breathe Believe Balance*. I am sure the book will benefit the readers in transforming their lives positively'

Gaur Gopal Das, author of *Life's Amazing Secrets*

'I am personally drawn to the manner in which this book blends spirituality with science. Inspiring, uplifting and thought-provoking. I wish I had read something like this twenty years ago'

Lara Dutta, actor and former Miss Universe

'Shayamal and I have experienced some extremely turbulent times in the high pressure of IPL and CPL cricket tournaments. A close mentor in High Performance, the lessons he shares in this book have helped me in personally reflecting on my past, present and future, and to rediscover my perspective in volatile times. *Breathe Believe Balance* is a must-read for anyone who is searching for equilibrium in life'

Brad Hodge, Australian Cricketer and former Head Coach, Kings XI Punjab, Saint Lucia Stars

'In *Breathe Believe Balance*, I found the answers to the big questions I was grappling with – how do I accept and learn to love myself, what is my purpose here, and how do I achieve balance both within myself and with the world around me? In short, a powerful, practical guide to self-discovery, healing and happiness that we all must read'

Soha Ali Khan, actor and author of *The Perils of Being Moderately Famous*

'This book is profound and sophisticated, yet simple to understand. It is spiritual and philosophical, yet very practical and well structured. It is gripping and it carries you all the way through ... If you want to GET balance, not KNOW or UNDERSTAND it, but get it on a cellular level so that it actually transforms your life, don't just read the book, keep this book as your tutorial to a fulfilled and balanced life'

Kristina Mänd-Lakhiani, Founder, Mindvalley

'In *Breathe Believe Balance*, Shayamal downloads twenty years of learning from his life in sports and spirituality. His insights on subjects like personal growth, mindfulness, and emotional healing are simple yet powerful'

Sania Mirza, former No. 1 WTA Tennis Professional and Padma Bhushan awardee

'A fabulous work by my good friend, Shayamal, who applies great dedication and his rich experience to educate us on the importance of reaching the optimal balance in life through a physical, mental, and spiritual approach in our daily lives and routines. Undoubtedly, you will find this book very useful on the way to your new and prosperous future'

Max Miryni, Olympic Gold Medalist and 10 x Tennis Grand Slam Champion

'This little but powerful book with its worksheets is your personal guide that handholds you as you work your way through life's growth and challenges. Each chapter is a gem in itself'

Amit Mookim, Managing Director, IQVIA

'A book like this can only be written by someone who has a deep understanding of the human condition and has a keen grasp of psychology, science, and spirituality. Vallabhjee is one such writer and life coach. He has given us a book that will help us to overcome our destructive patterns, find our strengths and lead fulfilling lives. We owe it to ourselves to get started on this "inner work" without delay'

Shunali Khullar Shroff, author of *Love in the Time of Affluenza*

Breathe
Believe
Balance

Shayamal Vallabhjee was born in Durban, South Africa. He is a sports scientist with a master's in Psychology. He has spent the past two decades working with Olympians, professional sports teams, corporate executives, patients, and children. Having lived as a monk in the Hare Krsna Temple, he now draws on learnings from ancient spiritual practices in combination with evidence-based science to help motivate and inspire people.

Breathe Believe Balance

A Guide to Self-discovery and Healing

Shayamal Vallabhjee

PAN

First published 2020 by Pan
an imprint of Pan Macmillan Publishing India Private Limited
707, Kailash Building,
26, K. G. Marg, New Delhi – 110 001
www.panmacmillan.co.in

Pan Macmillan, 6 Briset St, Farringdon, London EC1M 5NR
Associated companies throughout the world
www.panmacmillan.com

ISBN 978-93-89109-60-3

In this book, the author presents many powerful ideas to aid in your spiritual, physical and emotional healing. As with all books containing advice on health and healing of any kind, please seek the guidance of a licensed medical professional before implementing any of the techniques.

1 3 5 7 9 8 6 4 2

Typeset in Officina Sans Std by R. Ajith Kumar, New Delhi
Printed and bound in India by
Replika Press Pvt. Ltd.

To H. H. Bhakti Charu Swami, H. H. Radhanath Swami,
Mum and Dad

For lovingly guiding me in the service of Krsna

Contents

Introduction

Buddhism teaches that we move closer towards harmony once we accept that everything is in a state of impermanence. Harmony is an acceptance of our current reality and its relationship to our external environment.

Accepting impermanence, as a principle, was the toughest lesson I have ever learnt. If I may ask myself, was I ready to learn it? Absolutely not. As is true of life, we don't get to choose our battles, nor the time when we are to fight them. I struggled mentally, physically and spiritually to become the person I am today. By absorbing the lessons of these struggles, I embraced impermanence, became spiritually awakened, and understood what balance truly represents.

This book is the journey of how I found harmony, balance, and flow in my life. It is my personal blueprint of everything I have learnt in twenty years of my career as a sports scientist and High Performance Coach. Growing up in apartheid South Africa, I felt the pain of discrimination. The wounds have left a deep impact on my soul. There is a Japanese saying, *Ame futte ji katamaru*, which means, '*After the rain, the earth hardens.*' It is a poetic expression of how adversity builds character and makes you stronger. The saying also teaches you to be grateful for the struggles that make you who you are.

In this book, I have been honest, transparent, and emotionally vulnerable. If somewhere in your heart you are holding on to a dream of a better life, I am going to give you the tools that will help you become the person who can create that life. I have held nothing back. I know what pain feels like, and this is my honest attempt at giving you a chance to heal your own pain.

Balance is a word that has intrigued me all my life. Probably because very little of my life ever resembled balance. In school, I either failed or received an exemption. Then I chose a career that was the most unconventional, especially for a 'brown guy' in South Africa. When I realized that I needed to emotionally heal, I moved into a temple instead of consulting a therapist. I have even left the country to get out of a relationship. I train Olympians and professional athletes who are at the forefront of human potential, and in constant search of a competitive edge. And also work with terminally ill patients who are hanging on to every precious moment of their lives. When I decided to take up running, I wasn't happy with just marathons, I had to run ultra-marathons. And this narrative goes on.

In a sense, you might think that there is very little that I could ever contribute to a conversation on balance. Yet paradoxically, I was sure that somewhere in all my imbalances was the key to finding balance. In my heart I knew I just needed to understand the subject well enough, and dig deep enough, to find the needle in the haystack.

In spirituality one of the most powerful governing

principles is to identify that which is essential and eliminate the rest. By helping you tame distraction and reduce the noises in your mind, mindfulness enables you to see – more clearly – what is essential. And by acknowledging impermanence, you are able to let go of all that is transitory and inessential.

It is said that the moment you capture a butterfly and pin it down, it loses the very essence of what made it a butterfly in the first place. I feel much the same way about understanding balance. I have written this book as a guide to pursuing balance that respects the mystery and nuance of the subject. On the one hand, I want this book to be practical and usable and not so far up in your imagination that it becomes obscure or esoteric. On the other hand, I would want you to feel free – I don't want to pin down the butterfly to the point where it ceases to be a butterfly. Let's begin this journey!

Understanding the Brain

Finding balance needs a mindset shift. It has nothing to do with what you currently possess or other external circumstances, but rather with your perspective. If perspective is a by-product of your mental conditioning, then understanding how the brain constructs perspective is a great place to begin.

The human brain craves order, and that impulse is simultaneously a blessing and a curse. The brain's thirst for order expresses itself in four different ways. **It loves stories, symmetry, familiarity, and shortcuts.**

The brain dislikes anything random and accidental. If

you give your brain three unrelated facts, it will construct a narrative out of those facts. If you give the brain something it does not understand, in an attempt to comprehend it, it will carefully construct a story. As Lisa Cron puts it, humans and our brains are *'wired for story'*.[1] It is through stories that we understand and connect to (and make sense of) all that we taste, see, feel, smell, and hear.

The brain also prefers symmetry. Our desire for symmetry shows up in our art, our buildings, and our cities. Behavioural studies have confirmed that we are hardwired to see and seek symmetry. Exactly why that happens is somewhat of a mystery. It seems we use symmetry as a proxy or shorthand for well-being (sometimes this shorthand is accurate; sometimes not). More than anything, symmetry represents the familiar, and that is reassuring to the brain. Our deepest survival instincts all boil down to identifying danger. Although it doesn't always turn out to be true, our brains err on the side of caution and associate the unfamiliar with potential danger. For example, if a plant looks odd and unfamiliar, we do not eat it. In many cases these instincts have served us well, and so they have become wired into our brains.

Finally, the brain likes shortcuts. We are bombarded by more information than we can possibly process at a conscious level. We have hundreds of small decisions and judgments to make every passing minute. To deal with these demands our attention, our minds function in two modes: fast and slow.[2] The first works quickly and intuitively, relying heavily on association. The second is deliberate and methodical, but slow. Most of the times, we don't have the luxury of taking the slow route. We have to make a judgment immediately, and our fast thinking uses shortcuts to make those decisions quickly and efficiently. Most of the time those snap judgments are spot on. They have ensured our survival as a species. But, they can also lead us astray.

What does all of this have to do with this book and you?

We know that the brain craves order, but this desire for order isn't always our primal impulse. A deeper, more enlightened and spiritual impulse manifests in our pursuit of balance. Balance is more sublime and complex than mere order. Order is often static, but balance is alive and fluid. It is ultimately about harmony; harmony with ourselves, our environment, our fellow humans, the world, and the universe.

So, what is the problem? In our pursuit of balance, the brain's love of order kicks in, and the subtleties of balance go out of the window. We confuse balance with symmetry. Our brain's overwhelming desire for order leads us to oversimplify. Often, we fail to see the underlying balance in asymmetry. The result is that we try to impose a false sense of order on something that should naturally exist as fluid and dynamic.

I have spent the last two decades working with superhumans – athletes – who have cultivated the discipline and mastered the art of pushing their body and mind beyond the limits that constrain others. I have been the person tasked with optimizing their potential using evidence-based science and traditional medicine. In my quest to understand and optimize human potential, I studied physiology, psychology, spirituality, and alternative medicine. There were moments when I thought I had stumbled on the perfect solution. But over time that presumption faded, and I accepted that my ego was probably greater than the solution I had discovered.

There is no single reason why some athletes become superhumans. It is an intricate, dynamic balance between multiple domains that allows a chosen few to rise to the pinnacle of their potential. My thirst for knowledge sent me down the rabbit hole in search of the ideal balance. I did not find a single secret or formula. Instead, I was able to identify three broad principles that we must keep in mind during this journey:

1. the importance of mindfulness in balance
2. an appreciation for the fluidity of dynamic balance
3. the essential role of the fulcrum (point of support) in achieving balance

With these three principles as our north star, we can all find the balance that works best for us.

Ease versus Effort

Balance at times can be an elusive quality. Sometimes we are more acutely aware of its absence, a sense that something in our lives is missing or askew.

I want you to consider for a moment those times when one or more dimensions of your life were in sync – when you felt a sense of ease in any of the following:

- mentally (your relationship with your mind)
- physically (your relationship with your body)

- socially (your relationships with others)
- environmentally (your relationship with your surroundings)

Take a few minutes to sketch out the first memories that come to your mind. It is important to be able to tap into those memories, and to cultivate a kind of vivid muscle memory of that sensation. When we have experienced something and can recreate that experience in our mind, we know with confidence that we can recreate it in the future. This is what gives elite athletes an extraordinary edge. They have a sharply etched muscle memory – in their minds and bodies – of their previous triumphs under adverse circumstances. They draw on these memories to help them replicate a performance with ease and supreme confidence.

I specifically asked you to recall when you felt a sense of ease, because **ease is often a sign of balance.** A bicycle that is perfectly balanced seems to move through space without friction. A kitchen knife that is balanced cuts effortlessly. Great athletes have a finely developed sense of balance and it is one of the reasons they make difficult feats appear easy. Yoga is often called the art of balance, which shows in a trained yogi's fluid and graceful movements.

Conversely, imbalance often brings with it a feeling of great difficulty – a lack of ease. We may feel like we are slogging our way through mud: physically, mentally, or spiritually. Nothing seems to come easy. Even the smallest of things exhaust us. Ease and effort are often the most reliable indicators of the presence or absence of balance.

Understanding Imbalance Before You Can Change It

A recurring theme of this book is the importance of taking personal inventory: of our thoughts and emotions, of our body, of our relationships, and of the many dimensions of our lives. Imbalance can manifest subtly at first in our minds and then in our bodies. One of the reasons to practise mindfulness is that it allows us to be more alert to these subtle signs. When properly fine-tuned, both our minds and bodies are marvellous instruments. With mindfulness we can see the early signs of imbalance and take corrective steps.

Of major significance in this book is the ability to be emotionally mindful. When we are aware of our own thoughts and feelings, and those of others, we are better equipped to make clear and grounded decisions about the words we speak and the actions we take. This quality of *emotional intelligence*[3] is increasingly being recognized in the business world and elsewhere as a key factor in performance, success, and happiness. Mindfulness enables emotional intelligence; in turn, emotional intelligence allows us to live mindfully. As noted, Buddhist writer Jon Kabat-Zinn puts it, *'The real meditation is how you live your life.'*

We want to be cognizant of imbalance when it arises; but we also don't want to see imbalance when it isn't there. A good case in point is the work-life balance, a popular topic these days. On one hand, this term reflects some valid concerns. A workaholic who focuses single-mindedly on his or her profession – and at the expense of health, family, and relationships – is in most cases clearly not living in balance.

Yet, this is where our brain's preference for symmetry can

lead us astray. If we conflate symmetry and balance, we are tempted to picture work-life balance like a weighing scale, balance achieved only if the two sides look equal. This is an impossible standard for many of us, especially at certain stages of our lives. If you are fresh out of university, with no family obligations, happily working ten hours a day at a job you love, is your life out-of-balance? Not necessarily. If you are energized and fulfilled, you may be striking just the right balance for this moment in your life. The hours you spend at work and in private pursuits may be asymmetrical, but it is quite possible that there is an underlying balance to that asymmetry.

I often find myself searching for a different language, or other words – not necessarily to replace balance – but to bring nuance and other shades of meaning to it. Equilibrium is one such word that comes to my mind. It is a term often used to describe balance in dynamic situations, such as a natural ecosystem with many variables and moving parts.

For the sake of illustration, let's isolate two variables in such an ecosystem: a predator species (wolves) and a prey species (rabbits). Depending on the time of the year and the weather conditions, the population of each might rise and fall. An increase in rabbits would fuel a growth in the wolves' population, which would in turn cause the rabbits' population to fall. And it might take a relatively small number of wolves to keep a much larger rabbits' population in check. The two species are asymmetrical but in dynamic, moving balance with one another.

The same kind of things happen in our own bodies. Depending on when we eat and on our activity levels and other factors, our blood sugar level fluctuates throughout the day. In response, our insulin levels also fluctuate to keep our blood sugar from going too high or dropping too low. Just like the wolves and rabbits, the two are in dynamic, moving equilibrium.

Ecologists and biologists have both observed a kind of balance that is dynamic and multi-dimensional, as opposed to static and one-dimensional. I made the same discovery in my personal pursuit of balance.

Tough Lessons on Balance

As a young boy, I wanted nothing more than to be a professional cricket player. I grew up in Tongaat, a little town on the north coast of Durban in South Africa, a third generation South African of Indian descent. I was in love with the game of cricket, and for the better part of my childhood, I was consumed by the dream of playing cricket for my country. It took me more than a year to save up for my very own cricket kit – a possession I still hold on to today. When you grow up with humble means, even dreaming big seems like a crime. For me, I vividly recall how my devotion to the game of cricket threatened my relationship with my parents. It was only until much later that I realized they were only trying to protect me.

My cricketing dreams faced a formidable opponent: the system of institutionalized segregation and discrimination in South Africa known as apartheid. In the world of sports, apartheid took the form of a quota system which restricted the number of players of colour that could be represented on a team – even the national team. I was, at first, naively hopeful that I could overcome these odds. At the time, I suppose I was not sufficiently mindful[4] of how deeply discrimination was entrenched in South Africa. Eventually, I realized the quota system was a brick wall I could not hope to scale on my own. With my path blocked by such an unmovable obstacle, I had no choice but to take a different route.

I elected to pursue a degree in Sports Science, which to me felt like a happy marriage of various things I was already interested in. Yes, I had to give up the dream of my own athletic career; but I would be able to help others perform their best and could take vicarious satisfaction in their achievements. Sports Science would allow me to study biomechanics and exercise physiology in a rigorous and scientific way. I also had a natural interest in psychology. What makes people tick, what is the relationship between mind and body, how can we adjust our thinking to be happier and more fulfilled. Throughout the book, I draw on the insights I have gained through my studies, and my work with elite athletes and patients.

The reason I chose to study Sports Science went beyond just wanting to help athletes. Having faced the pain of discrimination on a personal way, I was determined to use any position I attained in the profession to make the world of sports free and fair. Sport is a true meritocracy – without class structure or inherited advantages. It is why we find competitive sports so compelling: we want to believe that anyone can triumph if they put their heart, mind, and soul into it. I wanted to make that ideal a reality and spare another aspiring young athlete from the heartache and discrimination I had faced.

What I didn't realize at the time was that I had discovered a key element of balance: we are more likely to perform at an optimal level when we are fighting for or representing something larger than ourselves. In their book *Peak Performance,* Brad Stulberg and Steve Magness write about the power of '*self-transcendence*' – not just in athletics, but in all walks of life. It is no accident that the first American to win the Boston marathon did so exactly a year after a terrorist attack marred the 2013 race. He wrote the name of the victims on his racing top; he was running for them as much as he was running for himself. A single village in Kenya produces almost half of the world's best marathon runners. Their secret sauce doesn't have much to do with diet or training, but with motivation: running is part of the town's identity, they run for one another.

While studying, I got a job to work with the state-level cricket teams in South Africa. I quickly progressed to the national teams, academies and high performance squads. I had a knack for discovering unique techniques to optimize training and recovery. I knew that if you could identify a key factor and measure it, you could improve it. It was only later that I came to fully appreciate the emotional and psychological dimensions of performance.

In 2003, I was hired to work for the Indian national team at the Cricket World Cup in South Africa. I was the team's technical analyst, responsible for studying the opposition, analyzing pitch conditions, and mapping data points that showed trends in performance. It was a life-changing experience for me. India made it all the way to the finals, but we unfortunately lost to Australia.

Following that successful world cup run, I felt I had a solid track record and resumé. I returned to Durban and interviewed for a job with the South African national men's cricket team. I was optimistic and was shortlisted as one of the final two candidates. After an hour-and-a-half interview, the then head coach came in and told me that he had flown in from Cape Town to appoint the other candidate. He wasn't even sure why I had been called in for the long interview, but I knew why. Despite my academic qualifications and my solid track record, I was just a token person of colour to fill a quota. I never had a chance.

I was terribly disappointed, of course. Despite everything I knew and had experienced about racism and discrimination, I wanted to give the system a chance; I sincerely believed my merit and worth would stand out. But more than that I was angry; I could feel a profound bitterness welling up inside me, and I could see quite clearly where that bitterness would lead me if I allowed it to take hold of me. Sadly, the system was not going to change anytime soon. In the meantime, I had to heal from the trappings of the apartheid.

At this point in my journey, **I had discovered another key to balance: harmony must exist not only between body and mind, but with the spirit as well. When something is missing or askew in our spirit, that imbalance will eventually derail us and throw us off our course** – regardless of what other elements of success are in place. We may outwardly look like we are thriving, but if our spirit is off-centre, our path is not sustainable. **Herein lies**

the difference between achievement and fulfilment. With will-power and drive, a good number of individuals may find some measure of achievement. But fulfilment requires a deeper balance: an alignment with some greater purpose.

In an attempt to rediscover my spirit, I turned to a temple where I had already spent a good deal of time: the Sri Sri Radha Radhanath Temple in Chatsworth, Durban. Having previously attended Bhagavad Gita classes and meditation sessions there, I knew the impact it would have on me. **Spiritual practice is the process by which we strip away distraction to reveal our true essence.** At first, I was not able (or ready) to leave all my worldly responsibilities. I reduced my workload significantly but hesitated to fully commit to monkhood. At a certain point I realized that bouncing between two worlds was preventing me from deeply immersing in either. I wanted my life in sports back, but I was consumed by the emotional pain of realizing that, no matter what I did, I was never going to be good enough. I had to make a decision for my sanity.

This is a good example of how tricky the question of balance is. At the surface level, I was making a decent effort to balance my real-world responsibilities with my exploration of a deeper spiritual practice at the temple. I was making a reasonable compromise by pursuing what appeared to be a middle path. But remember, **the brain sometimes confuses balance with symmetry**. At a fundamental level, I needed to commit wholeheartedly to my spiritual practice in order to find true balance. My life needed to be asymmetrical to enable the pursuit of a deeper balance.

And so, I made the decision to dive in with both feet

and to fully absorb myself in monkhood. The evolution was slow and exhausting; but with time, I could see that I had metamorphosed into someone compassionate, kind, and truly devoted to helping others transform. As a student of psychology, I had a deep appreciation for the ways spirituality gently but profoundly cultivates an individual's mindset. It was this journey into monkhood that led me to deepen my work in psychology and find a path that married spirituality and psychology.

In 2007, I left the temple and moved to India to train the Indian tennis team, that was preparing for the 2008 Beijing Olympics. By now, my spiritual training gave me the tools and the insight to address the question of balance in a far more sophisticated and nuanced manner. I was able to draw on the full range of my spiritual toolkit – physiology, psychology, alternative medicine, spirituality – in order to best serve an athlete at a specific point in time. I realized there was no formula to achieving world-class athletic success.

It was a big step for me, as a trained scientist, to move beyond that which was definitive and quantifiable. What matters, I learned, is not always what is measurable.

I spent six years on the ATP Tour with these professional tennis players. After the 2012 London Olympics, I set up a business in India called the HEAL Institute, which grew to be a multi-million dollar brick and mortar physiotherapy and physical rehabilitation business. It was conceptualized to raise the standard of care and education of non-surgical medical professionals working with sporting athletes.

If my career in sports science was born of my personal

experience of discrimination, the HEAL Institute was born of a different kind of discrimination. As I watched our Indian contingent prepare for the Olympics, my heart was heavy knowing how much the deck was stacked against them. They lacked access to state-of-the-art equipment, conditioning, nutrition, and technical analysis. I realized this was its own kind of discrimination and vowed afterwards to create a support system to prepare our athletes for world-class competition. HEAL was my attempt to help level the playing field for Indian athletes on a global stage.

The Japanese word *kinsugi* describes the art of repairing broken pottery with liquid gold: a symbolic representation of finding beauty in imperfection, and of celebrating the hardships that shape us. **When I look back at my pursuit of balance, it reminds me of how conflicted and paradoxical our attitude to growth is. We aspire for change and transformation. Yet, we often resist the struggle and challenges that produce such growth.**

At this moment in time, do I feel the sense of ease that accompanies balance? Absolutely yes. Do I think it will last forever? Absolutely no. Just as the wolves and rabbits have taught us, perhaps the best balance is found when you embrace the fluidity that accompanies a dynamic, multi-dimensional approach.

Let's Try a Thought Exercise

If I give you a length of board, a small but stable object like a metal cube to lay the board on, and two 1 kg weights, you can fairly easily arrange the weights on the board so they balance on the central point or fulcrum of the metal cube. If, instead, I give you a metal tube as a fulcrum, the balancing act becomes more difficult, but doable. If, on the other hand, I ask you to balance the weights with the board laid over a small water balloon, the task becomes nearly impossible. In each of these examples the only thing that has changed is the stability of the fulcrum.

This is both a practical example and a metaphor. The balancing act of life, more often than not, does not take place under stable conditions. Let's illustrate this further with a case from my own field of sports science and optimal performance.

When exercise machines like the Nautilus were introduced in the middle of the 20th century, they seemed like godsent for athletes, trainers, and fitness buffs. If you set yourself up correctly, the machine ensures that you have proper form, and that your spine and core are stabilized. You can push yourself to your limits without worrying about injury, or of dropping a weight on your toes. After an initial orientation, you don't even need a trainer or a workout buddy to spot you.

It turns out that exercise machines are fine if you just want neatly defined muscles, or if you need to isolate a specific muscle for the purposes of training or rehab. But if you want functional strength – that is, strength and agility in real-world competitive conditions – exercise machines have limited utility. Competition takes place in dynamic conditions where athletes must respond in a split second to the ball or the movement of an opponent. These dynamic conditions are usually inherently unstable; they force the athlete to create or restore his or her own stability and balance.

In recent times, professional athletes, trainers and consultants like me have gone back to old-school routines using free weights, medicine balls, and the body's own weight. In rehab or other kinds of narrowly tailored training, an exercise machine's ability to isolate a muscle can be useful. But in the flux and flow of competition, our muscles do not work in isolation, but as a complex, interdependent system. So, we now place a premium on training routines that exercise multiple muscle groups, and which force the athlete to engage their core and create their own stability.

Taking this example a little deeper, we realize that even these routines take place under relatively controlled and stable conditions, which is the opposite of what athletes face in competition. To counter this, we have devised tools and techniques that intentionally introduce instability. A prime example is the wobble board – not so different from the water balloon in our thought exercise. Standing on the wobbling board while trying to lift weights or throw and catch a medicine ball, the athlete creates their own shifting dynamic balance. They make constant micro-adjustments to stay balanced on the board. Facing an unstable fulcrum, their spine and core become a fulcrum unto itself.[5]

As this example illustrates, balance is a moving target. It is not a destination we find, and then let out a sigh of relief: *Good, I've got it; now I can relax.* In training and more so in competition, athletes are rarely in perfect balance. That is not the point or the objective. A tennis player lunging to return a volley into the corner is in an extreme state of imbalance. The question is: Do they maintain a certain stability and control amidst that imbalance? And how quickly are they able to restore balance?

Just like the tennis player, our lives are dynamic, with many moving parts, some of them beyond our control. Sometimes the very ground we stand on seems to move and shake – figuratively or even literally.

That brings us to another revealing illustration of dynamic balance. On 17 January 1995, the Hanshin region of southern Japan was hit by a devastating 7.3-magnitude earthquake. More than 6,400 lives were lost, virtually every structure within a seventeen-kilometre radius was damaged, and aftershocks were felt for more than two months after. It was the biggest national disaster in post-war Japan.

The disaster prompted Japan to explore and aggressively implement a rarely used technology called base isolation, that involves creating a buffer between the foundation and the rest of the building. During an earthquake, the foundation moves from side to side along with the ground, while the rest of the building remains relatively stable. This engineering technique represented an entirely new paradigm of structural stability – away from a fixed and static conception, and towards a more dynamic and fluid one.

Think of the athlete on the wobble board. If they try to maintain a perfect, fixed, static balance, they are likely to lose their balance entirely and fall. They learn, instead, to accept an imperfect, dynamic balance. Their lower legs will shake, but from the waist up they will remain remarkably stable.

Earlier we discussed the dynamic equilibrium of the body's metabolism as, for example, blood sugar and insulin levels rise and fall in conjunction with one another. The body is not striving for a fixed, static balance, but for what biologists call a *dynamic steady state*. Just like the athlete on the wobble board, or the building on its earthquake-proof base.

Now that you have a clearer sense of the difference between static balance and dynamic balance, let's look at the difference between one-dimensional and multi-dimensional balance and start by returning to the example of work-life balance.

The image that comes to mind when we think of work-life balance in its most simplistic form is of a weighing scale or maybe a board like in our thought exercise. By default, given the brain's affection for symmetry, we place the fulcrum in the middle. We place 'work' on one side, and 'life' on the other, and either they balance out or they don't.

This simplistic rendering of work-life balance ignores some fundamental realities about life in the real world.

- First, it is not a given that the fulcrum should be squarely in the middle. We have some say about where to position that fulcrum.
- Second, this image equates balance with symmetry. As we have seen, balance takes many forms. Sometimes balance *is* symmetry. At other times, balance is more like proportion: two things can be asymmetrical and yet in just the right balance with one another. At a certain point in your life, spending 80 per cent of your waking hours at work may be just the perfect proportion for you.
- Finally, this image reduces our life to a single dimension along a single plane. The reality is that our lives exist

along multiple dimensions, multiple planes. Just as no muscle in our body works alone and in complete isolation, but as part of a complex and interconnected system,[6] so the various aspects of our lives work together as an ecosystem in many ways. **Balance cannot be reduced to a single line.**

The Four Domains

Based on my research and studies, personal experiences, and work with world-class athletes, I have identified four major domains of our lives in which we should seek and cultivate balance.

BODY

Keys: Movement, Nutrition, Biological Age, Joint Health, Disease Prevention

- Are you able to control your body's inflammatory response?
- What is the quality of movement in your life?
- Are you able to live an enriching, restriction-free life?
- Are you able to control your body's glycemic variability?
- Is your heart healthy?
- Does your lifestyle leave you vulnerable to being diagnosed with chronic diseases?
- Are you eating healthy, organic meals?

- Are you conscious of where your food comes from?
- Do you struggle to sleep well?

MIND

Keys: Self-awareness, Mindfulness, Inner Peace, Empathy, Emotional Intelligence

- Are you in control of your emotions?
- Are you able to understand an emotion independent of the narrative behind it?
- Can you voice an opinion with love and compassion?
- How empathetic are you towards others?
- Are you able to maintain a positive outlook in life?

RELATIONSHIPS

Keys: Family, Lovers, Friends, Employees, Members of a Community

- Are you surrounded by individuals who nourish you?
- Are you aware of those relationships in your life that are toxic?
- Can you maintain a happy and healthy family relationship?
- Do you sometimes struggle to trust a loved one?
- Do you make friends easily?
- Are you comfortable being honest with the way you feel?

- Does the quality of your relationships suffer when you are under pressure?

ENVIRONMENT

Keys: Home, Workplace, Gym or field, Commute Distance, Ambient Noise

- How long do you commute to work?
- Is your work environment stimulating you?
- Are you rejuvenated when you get home?
- Do you derive personal satisfaction from your work?
- Are you able to see the impact you bring to the lives of others through your work?

The eight chapters that constitute the remainder of the book will help you examine and reflect on these four dimensions of your life. Hopefully they will also help you identify opportunities for creating greater balance. Each chapter will take you through a journey of introspection and retrospection.

A final question you may have after you are done is: **where do I start?**

There is no one answer, there is no formula. My work with high performance athletes offers some guidance to this question. Along this journey, I will share with you evidence-based scientific tests (many of which I use with my athletes) as well as life lessons from some of the world's greatest athletes and business minds. I hope you will find inspiration from the process and journey of others, including my own.

The initial step of the process is always inventory: thoroughly assessing all variables that might contribute to your success. The questions and thought exercises in the chapters that follow are expressly designed to help you familiarize yourself with the variables involved in your own pursuit of balance. In my work with my athletes, I go through a different kind of inventory to assist them in their pursuit of balance and athletic excellence. Before I develop a strategy to help them break through to the next level, I study more than three hundred physiological variables in combination with more than twenty psyche tests.

That kind of inventory might seem exhaustive and overwhelming, but in the end, I am just looking for two essential things. First, I want to identify the variable that provides the greatest leverage for change. In other words,

- where will concentrated effort yield the greatest results?
- where will my athlete and I get the biggest bang for our buck?

The second question complements the first. Searching for **the greatest leverage and the most far-reaching change often involves a degree of risk and experimentation.** We experience the deepest growth when we are on the edge of our comfort zones. And we need a measure of stability as a counterweight to that risk. The tennis player who lunges for a ball in the far corner of the court needs a stability point, a fulcrum for that extreme effort. And so, I also ask: **What variable provides my athletes with the greatest stability?** What is their home base, their anchor?

In everyone who has achieved great things in life, whether in sports or business or art or philanthropy, you will find this yin and yang, this dance between the risk and reach of change, and the necessary stability and grounding of a strong fulcrum.

Let's return to the thought exercise with the board and the water balloon. In that exercise, we learned about the importance of the fulcrum's integrity. The stronger the fulcrum, the easier it is to balance something on it. In life, you are the fulcrum. Each chapter in this book helps throw light on the variables that contribute to your physical, mental, spiritual, and social integrity. The stronger you are, the higher your probability of bringing the four domains (mind, body, relationships, and environment) into balance. The stronger your fulcrum, the further you can push yourself out of your own comfort zone. And the better your chances of maintaining a dynamic–steady state on the wobble board that is life.

Through the exercises in each chapter, you will cultivate an understanding of your strengths and the variables in your life that provide the greatest amount of support, emotionally and mentally. Knowing this is an important pre-requisite for balance.

An entrepreneur working sixteen hours a day can maintain this imbalance only if other components (relationship, body) are resilient enough to withstand the pressure.

In my personal life, I could push my physical and mental limits only because of my strong spiritual grounding.

If you want to find balance in life, two factors are non-negotiable: **the integrity of the self and a strong stable**

base in one of the four domains. If these are present, you are equipped to navigate balance in the most turbulent of environments.

Bringing it Home

I would like to close this introductory chapter with two fundamental principles. These are the major life realizations you will find sprinkled throughout the book.

Realization #1

You cannot heal that which you do not understand.

The pursuit of balance seems to be a universal one. Almost as universal is the sense that balance is somehow out of reach. As a student of life, a sports scientist, psychology-major, and former monk, I have dedicated my life to finding balance through science and spirituality. I have interviewed and mentored by innumerable philosophers, scientists, and gurus. I have questioned hundreds of thousands of individuals who are all in search of balance. Yet I have found almost no one – regardless of their level of achievement or success – who felt that they had attained balance. It is as if we are all in an episode of Indiana Jones or Tomb Raider, searching for something so elusive that we require a secret map to find it.

Could it be that no one has found balance because we are using the wrong map? Could it be that, in our quest for a balanced life, we have been set up to fail? *Could it be that our (mis)understanding of the very word balance is part of the problem?*

It was this insight that was the genesis of this book. I wanted to demystify balance but also to introduce some nuance to our vision of balance. When we confuse balance with symmetry, we are setting ourselves up to fail because we are striving for the impossible. The world is full of asymmetry, and so we must be able to find a balance within that asymmetry.

We also set ourselves up to fail when we strive for a balance that is fixed and static. **Life is fluid and dynamic, and so must be our conception of balance.**

Finally, our lives are multi-dimensional. We and the world we live in are complex, interconnected ecosystems. We cannot try to assess balance in a linear way, along a single dimension or plane. I have boiled down that multi-dimensional reality into four primary domains: body, mind, relationships, and environment. The chapters around which the rest of the book is written will allow you to fill out the map of your own journey towards greater balance. It will not be a straight line between points A and B, but something more complex, and hopefully more rewarding.

Just because that journey is not a straight line doesn't mean you have to get lost or overwhelmed. You have to start somewhere, by picking a variable you feel offers the greatest leverage for change. As you work on that variable, keep in mind the other dimensions of balance in your life: How they parallel one another, or in some cases intersect? Don't seek perfect symmetry between the areas of your life, but instead a ratio or proportion that works for you and that creates a feeling of harmony.

Realization #2

You cannot fix that which you are not prepared to change.

The questions that follow in this chapter will not only help you take inventory of the many variables in your life and how they do or do not contribute to balance – they will also help you assess your willingness to change. That willingness to change goes a long way towards establishing a solid fulcrum. You will have very little leverage without it.

Let's get a head start on that assessment by considering a question from each of the four primary domains of balance. For now, answer yes or no only.

Body: Are you prepared to change the food you eat to transform your life?
Mind: Are you prepared to change the way you think to transform your life?
Relationships: Are you prepared to change your relationships to transform your life?
Environment: Are you prepared to change where you live/work to transform your life?

Our willingness to change must be tampered with an acknowledgement of the difficulty of change. In my experience, the level of difficulty in effecting change in these four domains is as follows (going from easiest to hardest):

1. **Body:** Training and diet
2. **Mind:** Consistently re-engineering your thought process to manifest your new reality
3. **Relationships:** Cutting out toxic people from your life
4. **Environment:** You cannot heal in an environment that makes you sick

Keep this in mind as you read and ponder the questions that follow. They are designed to help you reflect and grow in specific areas of your life. Some are easier than others, but in the end they come together to help you flesh out a map in your pursuit of balance, a blueprint for life. As you identify areas for growth and work on making incremental gains, you will find yourself strengthening the integrity of your focal point, your fulcrum: YOU. You will find yourself able to create a dynamic balance that is nimble and adaptable to the flow and flux of life. You will develop an intuition for how to keep various areas of your life in optimal proportion to one another. You will realize that balance is a journey, a continual work-in-progress. Like a trained athlete, you will become more skilled at restoring balance and returning to equilibrium. The more you are in balance and equilibrium, the more you will experience that beautiful, fluid state in which your inner being is in harmony with your purpose and passion.

ONE

Self-love

(Mind, Body, Relationships, Environment)

1. What are the five things you love the most? (people, places, things)

Before reading this chapter, complete the list here. (Write down the first five things that come to your mind. Avoid overthinking the question)

1.

2.

3.

4.

5.

Once upon a time everybody had four legs and four arms, and one head with two faces looking in the opposite directions. These were whole people. But then, to make people weaker and less dangerous, the gods split them into halves. Only two arms and two legs each, like the people we see today. Some of these halves were men, and some were women. And from that moment, people started wandering all over, looking for their other half, hoping to become whole again. Sometimes your two halves are both men, and sometimes they're both women. Sometimes they're one of each.

This story, told by Plato (385 BC), is an evocative explanation of the origin of love. But the story is problematic in how it leads us to believe that we need someone else to feel complete – that until we find 'the one' we are destined to feel incomplete, lost, and unworthy.

This is a fundamental problem with society today. Many cultures, religions, castes, and classes have indoctrinated us to think that, without a partner, we are incomplete. Some go as far as to try to dictate exactly what the perfect union should look like, implicitly rejecting all who do not fit that mould. Beyond the question of romantic love, we are told in countless ways that we need something else to be complete: the right partner, the right job, the right house. We are told to look everywhere but the most obvious place: inside ourselves.

So, let's return to our thought exercise. **Where have you written down your name in the list?**

If your name does not appear on the list (which is all too common) that is a sign of self-neglect. Allow me to illustrate the cost of self-neglect with a story about a good friend, Gary, who was diagnosed with terminal lung cancer a couple of years ago.

Gary had been a smoker for more than thirty years. 'This was a long time coming,' he confessed to me. When I visited him at the hospital where he was receiving treatment, I bumped into Gary's family – his wife, their two girls who were now married, their husbands, and three grandchildren. As I walked into his room, Gary was wiping a tear from his eye.

'My family has been here with me in the hospital since the day I arrived. As much as I request them to not come, they are always sitting out there. My grandchildren and daughters should be out enjoying their lives,' he said, the tears rolling down his cheeks. 'Do you know, in thirty years of smoking, not a single person out of my family gave me a cigarette. They've done nothing to deserve having to go through this ordeal with me.' It was not the cancer that saddened him, but the effect it had on the lives of those who loved him. He realized, too late, that when we compromise the love and care of our own selves, we inevitably compromise the lives of those we love.

If you do not see yourself as a priority in your own life, you will never be able to commit to the actionable steps required to change your life and materialize your dreams. You will neglect yourself – your health, the quality of your thoughts, your relationships – and before long, you will even give up on your dreams. Why? Because the essence of self-love is self-respect; and when this is absent, it is difficult to prioritize your needs. You will neglect cultivating the strong inner sense of self that is your fulcrum, your basis for meaningful balance. The longer this pattern continues, the deeper it becomes embedded in your psyche. The Italian philosopher Thomas Aquinas was correct when he said, *'Each person should love himself and that such appropriate self-love serves as the basis for the possibility of giving oneself lovingly to another.'* But this is easier said than done.

The Greek hunter Narcissus was the son of the river god, Cephissus and the nymph, Lirope. Narcissus was extremely handsome, charming, and charismatic. His every movement was as graceful as a swan. His beauty was so captivating that everyone who laid their eyes on the young man immediately fell in love with him. Sadly, however, his soul and personality did not match his physical beauty. One evening, the young hunter was walking in the woods when he was spotted by the nymph, Echo. The little nymph immediately fell in love and tried to approach the young man, wanting nothing more than a hug. In his disdain, Narcissus pushed her away. The young nymph was overcome with despair and roamed the forest till she wilted away and all that remained was the sound of her echo.

Nemesis, the goddess of retribution and revenge, learned what had happened and decided to punish Narcissus for his behaviour. She led him to a pool where the young man saw his reflection in the water and fell in love with it. Spellbound by his own beauty, he did not at first realize it was just a reflection. When he finally understood this, he despaired that the reflection would never return his love, and he eventually committed suicide.

The mythological story of Narcissus reminds us of the dangers of being self-centred and lacking empathy and consideration for others. And yet, *narcissism should not be confused with authentic self-love.* Indeed, without a mindful approach to personal growth, it is easy to cross over from one to the other.

So, let's clearly define and distinguish between the two.

Narcissism *is a personality disorder where an individual has a dangerously inflated sense of self-importance, often resulting in a total lack of empathy towards those around them.* A tell-tale trait is the narcissist's fragile mental state, a need for constant reassurance of their self-worth.

Self-love, *on the other hand, is a cultivation of one's self-worth and a healthy acceptance of one's achievements and personality.* In raising our vibrational energy, we construct a strong foundation on which we can create, nurture, and support healthy, meaningful relationships around us.

In my own effort to truly understand self-love, I turned to the words of Aristotle, who contemplates the connection between love and the relation to self as follows: *'True friendship is possible only between virtuous people, and so only between people whose natures are formed.'* He goes on to say: *'Love of others proceeds from a good man's relation to himself.'*

Aristotle touches critically on the **role of virtues in the cultivation of a relationship**. If this sounds like a reach, think back to those times when you had a reason to discontinue a friendship with someone. If you dig deeply enough, you will invariably find a breach in the core values you thought you shared. A breach in values is like a fault line in a building, or in the earth itself. Once that fissure appears, the structure is doomed to split and crumble. As the Bible says, *'A house divided against itself cannot stand.'*

This applies to our relationships with others, and our relationship with ourselves. Aristotle beautifully highlights how an individual's virtues help him or her form meaningful bonds. In turn, for us to love ourselves, we must first understand and appreciate our own inner virtues. In approaching the self as a discrete entity, we can learn to be mindfully aware of what it is we love about ourselves, why we love these qualities, and how they enrich our lives and the lives of others. In other words, we approach that relationship with ourselves as we would any other friendship.

Understanding Core Values/Virtues

A **core value** by definition is a fundamental belief system or guiding principle that dictates behaviour, and helps individuals distinguish between right and wrong.

To identify what core virtues or values truly resonate with you, I encourage you to answer the following questions. Try to be as exhaustive as you can with each question, and answer them using descriptive words or phrases only.

1. Which qualities have contributed the most to your success?
2. How would you like to be remembered when you leave a room?
3. What part of your job do you love the most?
4. What is the most rewarding feeling you give to others?
5. What qualities are you most proud of?
6. What do others say you are good at?

Here is a partial list of core values and virtues that you could choose from. This is only a guide and you are in no way obligated to use any of these, though it may help you describe an emotion or feeling that resonates with you.

Dependability	Reliability	Loyalty	Honesty	Consistency
Positivity	Respect	Environmentalism	Humour	Innovation
Education	Perseverance	Courage	Adventure	Passion
Love	Service	Integrity	Authenticity	Compassion
Leadership	Trustworthiness	Knowledge	Security	Freedom

After you answer each of these questions, you will notice there are a few common words or phrases. Some of these may be generic, and some very specific to you as an individual. I would encourage you to remove those generic words (kindness, friendly, happy).

Then, begin to pool together the common words and phrases. Sometimes, you may need to group a few words that could mean the same thing. Try to keep grouping words till you get 4-5 key values or virtues. These would represent the first iteration of your core values.

As a final step, I would encourage you to look at the various definitions of each word. Perhaps there is a synonym that better represents that value in your life. You can swap those words. Sometimes, upon reflection, a certain value might not resonate with you completely. Feel free to remove it. If you want to start with just one or two values, that is perfectly okay.

Remember, these values represent who you are now and not the future version of yourself.

This brings me to the third realization.

Realization #3

You cannot love yourself if you hate the experiences that have made you the person you are.

In 2012, I started a healthcare business in India. Five years later, this booming business was poised to raise its first round of institutional funding. The documentation process went well but before the infusion of funds, my investors threw me a curve ball. They wanted to pivot the business from a niche healthcare brand to a mass market brand. I resisted at first; but, given their stranglehold on the funding,

I was backed into a corner. My only choices were to give in or step away. The decision to step away was not as difficult as I initially expected, but with time I learnt that those wounds cut deeper than I realized.

I took a one-year sabbatical, during which I penned down a book on entrepreneurship, started a new digital media business and relaunched my speaking career. On the surface I was moving forward, but an undertone of resentment and an uneasiness would creep in me in the most unexpected of situations. Beneath the surface, unresolved emotions simmered: a sense of betrayal, guilt for having walked away from something I had built, unspoken excuses for why I could not speak about my journey on stage, and an inability to trust my new partners.

Everything pointed in one direction. *I had not accepted and healed from that loss and hurt. I was showing the world one version of myself while my inner true self was in conflict.* I lacked alignment because I refused to accept the outcome of an experience. I took my own journey of retrospection and questioned myself about other instances of trauma I had experienced. Had I truly acknowledged, accepted, and healed from them? Apartheid. Unfaithfulness. Losing a loved one, and the list goes on.

If I had not healed from these experiences, how could I be grateful for them? If I was not grateful for them, how could I accept who I am today? If I cannot accept who I am today because of my inability to love the experiences that made me who I am, how can I learn to love myself?

My failure to grapple with my past amounted to a degree of self-sabotage of my present life. I had to look squarely at my past, and to heal from it.

In order to navigate my own journey from hurt to healing to self-love, I came up with my **SAFE Method:** *a four-step process by which we become aware of negative experiences in our lives, understand and acknowledge the feelings that spring from them, shift our mindset towards forgiveness, and lastly, recreate habits and patterns that raise our vibrational energy and enlighten our soul.*

The SAFE Method

S – Self-examine

In the words of the writer Ralph Ellison, *'When I discover who I am, I'll be free.'*

Self-examination is the process of cultivating self-awareness: the ability to understand **what** we are doing at the precise moment we are doing it, along with an awareness of **why**. This may seem like common sense, but most of us are driven by subconscious fears and impulses, and we act on those buried emotions without being aware of them. Self-examination brings our hidden emotional life out of the shadows and into the light.

A – Acknowledge and Accept

Suppressed emotions are like stagnant energy that binds you and holds you back. Once we cultivate self-awareness and bring these suppressed emotions to the surface, the next step is to acknowledge and accept them. When you acknowledge and feel an emotion, you convert that stagnant energy to kinetic energy, an energy we can use to transform ourselves. Acceptance, in turn, allows us to fully feel the difficult emotions we have tried to bury in the past. We must let those emotions flow before we can let them go.

F – Forgive

If anger is a burden we carry over someone else's mistakes (or our own) forgiveness is the compassion we grant ourselves and others when we release that burden. Forgiveness is the process by which emotions are first acknowledged and felt, and then released and transformed into a new healing energy.

E – Energize and Elevate

In the forgiveness phase, we release the shame, blame, and anger that prevented the best version of our self from flourishing. We learn to see light in what was previously a dark tunnel. In this fourth phase, we focus on activities that raise our vibrational energy. We take a journey inward to heal the wounds of our past and enjoy the benefits of self-love and self-care. By focusing on our inner self, we cultivate virtues of kindness, compassion, self-esteem, self-confidence, love, empathy, and passion. As Aristotle suggested, when we identify positive virtues within, it becomes easier to cultivate a loving friendship with ourselves.

Before we dive deeper into the SAFE Method, let me briefly share the story of one of my patients, Mary. In her mid-thirties, she was going through a divorce after just a few years of marriage. Despite recently having a child, she was convinced that her husband was unfaithful. When I asked her to describe the events that convinced her of this, she spoke of each incident with anger, impatience, frustration, and disgust: the emotions of a person in a fixed emotional state. When we fully acknowledge and accept our emotions, we move through them and thus, our emotional states become fluid. When we are governed by subconscious emotions of fear, anger, and shame, we become stuck in a given emotional state – which in turn becomes a fixed state of mind that alters our very perception of the world. An unresolved problem from the past becomes the lens through which we view our present and future. Fixed emotional states are a sign that we lack mindful awareness of our emotions.

I asked Mary to understand her emotions, to identify the patterns and triggers behind them. The SAFE Method allows us to bring mindfulness to an experience. Mindfulness is intentional awareness. Without intention, our awareness is like water. If you pour water into a plant, it will nourish both the plant and the weeds. It does not distinguish between the two. Without mindful awareness, our mental state (for reasons I will explain further) actually gives preference to and fixates on negative emotions.

Mary was stuck in a negative cycle of self-sabotage and pity – a cycle linked to a particular narrative, a story she told herself over and over again. The brain likes stories, and sometimes we get stuck in them. Mary was at first unable to separate her emotions from this narrative playing on a loop in her mind. The SAFE Method taught her to understand and accept her emotions independent of this narrative. She found clarity, and from there, healing was only a matter of time.

Mindfulness is the process by which we intentionally draw our awareness to a particular moment, and to the emotions that experience generates. With practice, we can become a non-judgmental witness to the experience, and truly understand and embody the emotions we are feeling. We bring buried emotions and triggers into the light. Our view of the world is no longer governed by fixed emotional states, and we can see the world as it is, with an open and accepting heart. Without such mindfulness, your mind becomes a breeding ground for the most toxic and destructive emotions.

If you are ready now, we can begin our work with the SAFE Method:

You can read through these pages to understand and absorb the methodology, but when you are starting to work through a personal experience, please retreat to a quiet, safe space. Healing is tough and will require your undivided attention and focus. You are welcome to practice a little mindfulness (focusing on your breath) to help centre your energy.

Remove all distractions from the room and keep a glass of water close by.

Lastly, during the first few minutes of your mindfulness practice, set an intention for the work you are going to be undertaking. This could include: viewing an experience from a different perspective, feeling the associated emotions, being a witness to the experience, and being open to channeling new solutions. Defining intent is a way to define the world you would like to create. It is your personal playground of possibilities.

1. Self-examination:

In the 1960s, the American neuroscientist and psychologist Paul MacLean became a sensation with his theory of what he called the 'triune' (or three-part) brain. In his model, the brain consisted of a reptilian or primal brain, that focused on survival; our limbic system or emotional brain; and our neocortex, our thinking, rational brain. His ideas were popularized by the famous astronomer Carl Sagan, and they had an enormous cultural influence.

The theory of the triune brain has since been superseded by a more sophisticated understanding of how the brain functions, but MacLean's ideas were a useful step forward.[1] Psychologists like Jung and Freud had long theorized about the importance of the unconscious and the subconscious; MacLean's theory was neuroscience's first attempt to relate these earlier insights to an objective understanding of the brain. His major contribution was to remind us of the extent to which our thoughts and emotions are grounded in the unconscious and subconscious, and how much these thoughts and emotions are tied to primitive survival instincts.

From an evolutionary perspective, it turns out our emotions are first and foremost designed to protect us. They are intimately connected with our primal flight-or-fight response to potential danger. As writer, Bessel van der Kolk puts it, '*These raw, instinctive emotions are our brain's smoke detector*[2] *– responsible for identifying fear and preparing our body for an emergency response.*' For this reason, as I mentioned earlier, the brain seems to naturally fixate on fear-based emotions.

These survival-based instincts can save us, but they can also sabotage us. When our emotional states are ruled by subconscious fears, our minds can get, in the words of Daniel Goleman, 'hijacked' by our emotions. Goleman is a pioneer in the field of positive psychology, introducing us to the essential idea of *emotional intelligence*. The goals of emotional intelligence and the SAFE Method are the same: retrieving buried emotions from the shadows and into the light.

Having said that, **the following thought exercise can be applied to any experience, memory or emotional state** you feel may be holding you back. This self-examination is the first essential step to emotional healing.

As stated before, allow yourself time and space to reflect deeply, and be gentle with yourself:

1. Think of a situation or experience that has been troubling you.

2. What are the emotions you feel when you think about this experience?
3. Are you in control of your thoughts, emotions, and vocabulary when you think about this experience?
4. Have you experienced a similar situation before? Is there a pattern?
5. Do you make excuses for the situation?
6. Have you attempted to view this situation from multiple perspectives?
7. What are some of the interventions you have tried to rectify the situation?
8. Do you feel important when you speak about this situation?
9. Do you feel this experience explains certain things missing from your life?
10. What have you learnt from this experience?
11. Do you find yourself speaking to others who have had similar experiences?
12. What are you open to changing in an attempt to change this situation?

There are no right or wrong answers. These questions are simply a framework for diving deeply into an experience, and for developing your own emotional intelligence. You might feel, as I have, an urge to skim through your responses to these questions the first time you start to put them down on paper. I would urge you to spend time and explore the depths of each question. Remember, we are attempting to understand our pain from conscious, subconscious, and unconscious points of view. There are thoughts on the surface (conscious), feelings just below (subconscious), and instinctive physical and emotional triggers below that (unconscious). Like peeling away layers of an onion, the deeper you go, the tougher it gets.

How we feel about a situation has an extremely powerful influence on our health. For this reason, developing the courage to delve into our inner selves is essential for healing. In addition to bringing much-needed awareness to the pain you are feeling, such introspection also highlights the subconscious triggers and blocks that prevent you from healing and from manifesting the future you want.

If I had to put it simply, lack of awareness is our biggest stumbling block to healing.

2. Acknowledgement and Acceptance:

I introduced the theory of the triune brain because it is a window into the power of our subconscious. Acknowledgement and acceptance is the second stage of the process of bringing hidden emotional hurt to the surface and into the light where we can find closure and healing. In the last section, I talked about how buried emotions are a kind of stagnant energy that blocks and prevents us from healing and evolving. It also becomes internalized psychically (in the form of negative emotional patterns) and physically (in the form of disease).

Blocked trauma and invisible emotional patterns translate directly into behaviour and self-defeating habits by way of triggers. Basically, our subconscious emotional states become hard-wired into us like a computer programme, and are then activated by small cues and stresses in our everyday lives. This happens automatically, out of sight (and almost out of mind).

The same process happens on the physical plane as well. I have spent the better part of a decade working with patients to unlock the subconscious emotional traumas that lead to diseases like cancer, autoimmune disorders, and chronic pain. **On both the physical and the psychological levels, simply being aware of the underlying emotional state can lead to significant improvements in mood and health.** This has been confirmed by brain-mapping studies at the University of California and elsewhere. Participants who were able to name a negative emotion showed less activity in the amygdala (our emotional alarm centre) and more activity in the prefrontal cortex (our conscious, rational brain).

In September 2018, a patient in India approached me with a type of Hodgkin's Lymphoma in the chest. He had been suffering for more than six months. When I questioned him about any emotional trauma that he was experiencing, he at first struggled to put his finger on any emotional situation that could have resulted in his diagnosis. I explained to him that while Hodgkin's Lymphoma in the chest can be caused by genetic predisposition, it can also be triggered by underlying emotional conditions involving a lack of self-worth, and that it made sense to explore a possible emotional trigger first.

This young man was immediately able to identify the relevant emotional trigger: a recent entrepreneurial success he felt to be undeserved. A startup of his was booming beyond expectations, and for no clear reason; and that unexpected success had created a false sense of self-worth. With this fame came the fear that it may be gone one day, and with it his identity.

When we acknowledge that our thoughts, beliefs, and emotions are psychological levers that control everything in our lives, including our physical health, we give ourselves the power to change our reality. The work of Dr Masaru Emoto reveals how our thoughts and intentions have the potential to impact the physical realm. In his book *The Hidden Messages in Water*, Dr Emoto demonstrates how water exposed to loving, benevolent, and compassionate human intention results in aesthetically pleasing physical molecular formations in the water, while water exposed to fearful and discordant human intentions results in disconnected, disfigured, and 'unpleasant' physical molecular formations.

If our thoughts can impact the quality of a water molecule, can you imagine the impact they have on every cell in our body?

Acknowledgement and acceptance is an inward journey whereby you become conscious of yourself. There is no questioning the fact that healing is tough. The process of cleansing out the conscious, subconscious, and unconscious triggers that do not serve us is difficult work. Most individuals struggle to do so, because we cannot cleanse that which we do not acknowledge or recognize.

The steps I am delineating mirror the process of grieving described by psychiatrist Elisabeth Kubler Ross in her book *On Death and Dying*. Anyone who has undergone some emotional trauma has experienced **the five stages of grief** that she has identified as **denial, anger, bargaining, depression,** and **acceptance**. In a sense, when we dig up buried emotional trauma, we are learning to grieve over unresolved pain and disappointment from the past.

Below are some **questions to guide you in this process of acknowledgement and acceptance**. As always, allow yourself adequate time and space for this difficult work:

1. As with the last series of questions, identify a situation or experience that has been troubling you.
2. Are you able to understand and interpret the emotions you are feeling?
3. On a scale of 1-10, how clearly can you recognize the emotions?
4. Can you precisely interpret all the underlying emotions without being consumed by the narrative?
5. How does each emotion make you feel physically? Can you feel it in a specific place in your body?
6. Do you recognize the duality in each emotion? For example, in a moment of sadness, can you imagine its opposite?
7. Are you resisting the emotion or are you able to accept it?
8. How long can you hold and absorb the emotion?
9. Can you visualize each emotion evolve? What does this feel like?
10. Would you feel comfortable expressing this emotion?
11. If you hold your awareness on the emotion, do you feel your body relax or tense up?

The acknowledgement and acceptance of an emotion is challenging. It is especially difficult in a world of distraction and noise. In order to heal, we have to mindfully step away from distraction and into self-awareness.

3. Forgiveness

If you walk into my office, there is a quote that hangs on the wall. The exact same quote can be found in all of my offices.

> *'There is no future without forgiveness.'* – Desmond Tutu

I grew up in South Africa during the apartheid era. The oppression, segregation, injustice, and discrimination cut through the dreams of every person of colour like a hot knife through butter. If I had not lived through that time and personally witnessed how Mandela galvanized a divided nation with forgiveness, it would read like a story too good to be true. If you want to understand the power of forgiveness, look no further than the remarkable example of Nelson Mandela. A prisoner who became the president, who then worked diligently to propagate love and forgiveness as he unified his country. As he said, *'Forgiveness liberates a soul, it removes fear. That is why it is such a powerful weapon.'*

Every philosopher associates forgiveness with liberation. Liberation by definition is the act of setting someone free from imprisonment, slavery, or oppression. Have you ever wondered why they choose to pair these words together?

Without forgiveness, you are imprisoned by your past. You are a victim to the pain inflicted on you by someone else. In the chapters to come, I address the dangers of a victim mentality. What makes a victim mentality so dangerous is that it renders you powerless to change the situation. In Buddhist philosophy, forgiveness is understood as means to end our suffering. It brings dignity and harmony to any situation; and, contrary to popular belief, it is not a sign of weakness. It is a sign of strength and courage. You could think of forgiveness as the pathway to redemption from your past.

A Buddhist Lesson on Forgiveness

A young man was walking down a narrow road when he was hit by a stone. He turned around and saw the boy who had thrown the stone. The man was furious. A Buddhist monk sitting nearby watched the entire incident unfold. He called the young man over.

Monk: *Why are you angry?*

Man: *This young boy threw a stone at me.*

Monk: *So, are you angry at the boy or the stone?*

Man: *I am angry at the boy.*

Monk: *But it was the stone that hit you, not the boy.*

Man: *Yes, but the stone had no intention of hitting me. It is an inanimate object. The boy threw it at me, so I am angry at him.*

Monk: *Well, if we use your logic. You should not be angry with the boy as well. You should be angry with his pain. That boy is just like the stone. He was helplessly thrown by his pain.*

The Buddhist monk was teaching the young man that much of our behaviour is controlled by our perception. Often we are unable to see the triggers that control our lives and our actions. Realizing how an individual's actions are at times controlled by those subconscious triggers makes it easier to show them compassion and forgiveness. If we can draw our attention even deeper, we will realize that our own actions are also governed by similar triggers we may not be aware of. We too, are vulnerable to our triggers. At times, we may also become a victim of a trigger, causing us to behave in an unbecoming manner. **Wouldn't it be nice if we were shown compassion and forgiveness in that moment?**

To assess our ability to view a situation from a different perspective, we can perform:
The Five P's Exercise – which involves answering the following questions:

1. **Pressure:** Could there have been situational pressures that made an individual behave in a particular manner?
2. **Past:** What were the background factors that contributed to them behaving as they did?
3. **Personality:** What are the events in their lives that could have contributed to the personality they exhibit?
4. **Provocations:** What did I do that could be perceived as provocation?
5. **Plans:** What were the person's good intentions? Did they want to help me in some way, even though their actions did not have that effect?

A group of researchers randomly assigned 149 divorced individuals to a secular forgiveness group, a religious integrated forgiveness group, and a wait-list control group. The groups engaged in discussions around feelings of betrayal, coping with anger, forgiveness education, preventing relapse, and closure. It probably will not come as a surprise that participants in the groups reported higher levels of forgiveness and lower depression than the wait-list group. Research like this has resulted in a number of innovative programmes pioneering the use of forgiveness to alleviate long-standing suffering, pain, and conflict.

In *The Art of Forgiveness: Differentiating Transformational Leaders*, Manfred Kets De Vries walks us through a **Forgiveness Questionnaire** designed to help you understand your capacity to forgive. Here is the questionnaire:

Please answer the following questions as honestly as you can. Rate each item on a scale of 1 to 5. Circle the appropriate number.

1 = Strongly disagree
2 = Disagree
3 = Neutral
4 = Agree
5 = Strongly agree

1.	I continue to behave negatively towards someone who has done something that I think is wrong	1	2	3	4	5
2.	If someone does something bad to me, I will retaliate	1	2	3	4	5
3.	I will continue to be unpleasant towards others who have hurt me	1	2	3	4	5
4.	I find it very difficult to overcome bad situations in my life	1	2	3	4	5
5.	If others mistreat me, I will think poorly of them	1	2	3	4	5
6.	I hold onto grudges and negative feelings over perceived wrongdoings	1	2	3	4	5
7.	I do not need much provocation to get back at another person	1	2	3	4	5
8.	I will continue to feel resentful even if the offender has asked for forgiveness	1	2	3	4	5
9.	I am not really the forgiving type	1	2	3	4	5
10.	I find it difficult to accept any remorse and sorrow expressed by others for their actions or words that have hurt or disappointed me	1	2	3	4	5
11.	I often feel that I have had a rough deal in life	1	2	3	4	5
12.	I strongly believe that if someone makes a mistake, or acts wrongly, there should be consequences	1	2	3	4	5
13.	I seem to get into arguments more often than other people	1	2	3	4	5
14.	I often feel very resentful about things	1	2	3	4	5

15.	I find it very difficult to let go of grievances	1	2	3	4	5
16.	I am always on my guard against people who may hurt me	1	2	3	4	5
17.	It would be very difficult for me to forgive my partner if I thought that he/she had betrayed me	1	2	3	4	5
18.	I would find it hard to forgive a colleague if he/she took advantage of me	1	2	3	4	5
19.	I would find it very difficult to let go of anger and hatred	1	2	3	4	5
20.	I don't have the kind of worldview that welcomes forgiveness	1	2	3	4	5

If you arrive at a score of 40 or less, you belong to the group of people who are truly forgiving. If you score 80 or above, forgiving is something that doesn't come naturally to you. You will be a happier person, however, if you work on your ability to forgive and let go.

If you score between 40 and 80, you belong to the group of people who are able to forgive, but not without difficulties.

Forgiveness is a gentle process that must be approached with love, kindness, and patience. Remember, it is possible that we have been carrying the emotional pain for a long time. With this pain, we may have become numb to emotion, or worse, built walls around us to protect us from being hurt again. Forgiveness is not only about recognizing the pain we are feeling, but also the processes we have subconsciously created for self-preservation. Some of these processes may take the shape of self-sabotaging self-talk. You may recognize them in statements such as 'I am never going to let anyone hurt me again,' or 'I do not need anyone.' None of these processes serves us well.

Using the Five P's and the Forgiveness Questionnaire, you will be able to understand how ready you are to extend forgiveness to yourself and others. It will allow you to bring enough mindfulness to the trauma and begin the healing process. Nothing about healing is easy, but ignoring our pain cuts deep wounds, the scars of which become more painful to deal with than the initial trauma.

The evidence is overwhelming. As humans, we have evolved to connect through positive emotional experiences. Because of our innate need to connect, there is an apparent forgiveness window (a specific time frame) during which most errors in judgment can be rectified. The only stumbling block in exploiting this window of opportunity is our ego. It turns out that the longer we feed this beast, the stronger it becomes. **Forgiveness has the power to transform our emotional life, our health at the cellular level, and society itself.** It is for this reason that it is such an essential part of the SAFE Method.

4. Energize and Elevate

An optimist sees a glass as half full.
A pessimist sees it as half empty.
And the wise sees the space that was being held for something more.

In the forgiveness phase, we release the negative feelings that prevented the best version of our self from thriving. We use our awareness to transform our perspective of the incident that previously caused us so much pain. We are now free to take what was previously stagnant energy and put it to good use.

> *'If you want to find the secrets of the universe, think in terms of energy, frequency and vibration.'* – Nikola Tesla

This leads us to my fourth realization:

> **Realization #4**
>
> *Everything you attract in your life is based on your own vibrational energy.*

Let's start by breaking down different ways of looking at and measuring energy.

Frequency: The number of occurrences of a repeating event per unit of time.

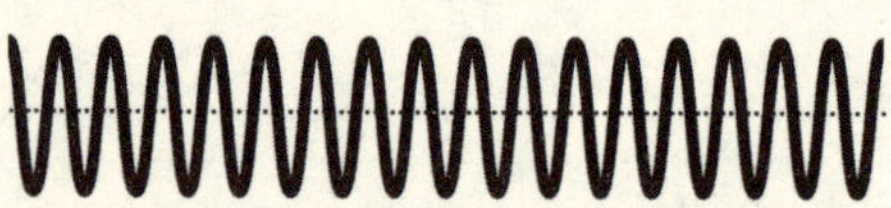

High Frequency

Low Frequency

Resonance: The amplification (the process of making a signal stronger) that occurs when the frequency of two vibrating objects are in harmonic proportions. Through resonance, the amplitude of a frequency can be raised.

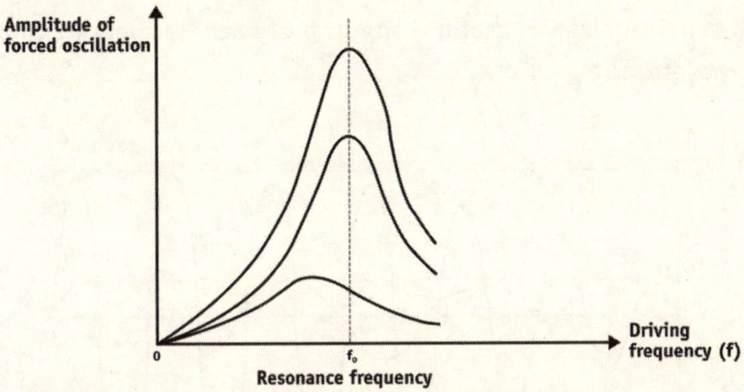

All things in our universe are in constant motion. Even if they appear stationary, they are in fact vibrating or oscillating at different frequencies. Everything in the world, animate or inanimate, is vibrating. However, for something to have a clear frequency, it needs to have a constant vibration. Whilst it is true that everything is vibrating, it is not true that everything has a constant frequency. Some human beings have a powerfully high frequency. For example, in the presence of someone who is spiritually awakened, you feel lighter, calmer, more blissful. You are picking up on a vibration and energy linked to consistent spiritual practice. Others have a low frequency, and in many cases, because of the inconsistency in their vibrational energy, they lack a frequency altogether. In the chapter on environments, I explain at length the relationship between different mental states and its impact on the environment.

Through resonance, the possibility of healing gets exciting. As I mentioned, resonance occurs when two vibrational frequencies harmonize or match. It is through this harmonization that the strength of each frequency signal gets stronger.

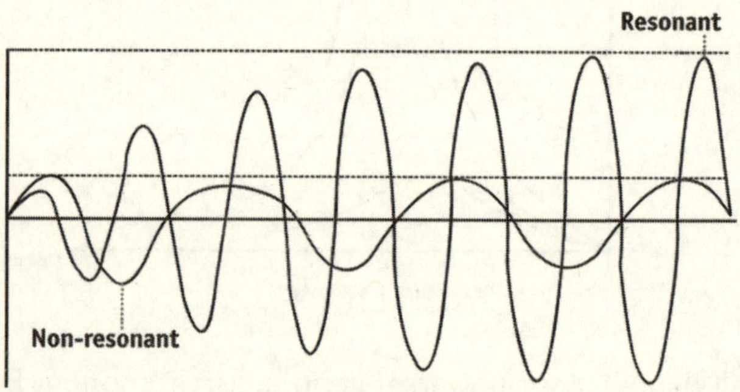

So why is all of this important to your healing journey?

Emotional trauma can be very disorientating. You might feel as if you are on an emotional rollercoaster, being thrown from side to side by your pain. Repetitive patterns and subconscious programmes can consume your mental space and physical energy. This results in inconsistency in every facet of your life.

Self-examination, Accepting and Acknowledging, and Forgiveness (from the SAFE Method) will help you bring awareness to the destructive patterns that were consuming you. Now that you have started to deconstruct past traumas and have begun your journey of healing, raising your vibrational energy is the catalyst to further evolving in every aspect of your life.

We must learn to become mindful of the power of associating with conscious, spiritually awakened souls who can raise our own vibrational energy. Through synchronization with these high-frequency souls, energy and information will flow more readily, resulting in a deeper, more intimate connection with others, and ourselves. Within these connections is the secret to healing, growth, and personal transformation.

You can learn to elevate your own energy by way of a simple four-step process:

1. Find your consistent frequency by incorporating a healing process into your daily routine.
2. Associate with individuals and groups who operate at a higher frequency.
3. Clean your diet. Food has vibrational energy and some foods support the healing process more than others.
4. Find a consistent time to sleep and wake up, ensuring that you get at least five sleep cycles per night.

How do you find a Consistent Frequency?

Here are my Top 10 ways to cleanse and raise your vibrational energy:

1. **Solitude Practice:** Most people find it difficult to meditate, chant, or do breathing exercises every day. If you are someone who cannot be consistent with

these practices, I recommend getting comfortable with solitude by spending at least twenty minutes alone daily (with no distractions of mobiles, TV, books, or newspaper).

2. **Daily Gratitude Practice:** Spend five to ten minutes a day (preferably at the same time) reflecting on all the people, situations, and other things that enrich your life. Gratitude practices hone our thoughts and allow us to shift our mindset and energy to something positive.
3 **Time in Nature:** Spending time around plants, trees, and grass can help provide energetic rejuvenation. They are a symbol of balance, fertility, and stability.
4. **Declutter Your Life:** Clutter prevents the flow of energy. It stagnates growth, creates blockages in energy, and results in a state of destructive imbalance. Cleansing your space and eliminating toxic relationships will help you heal faster and bring harmony into your life.
5. **Food is Medicine:** Different foods have different vibrational energies associated with them, which is why you are what you eat. In order of highest to lowest vibrational energy, these are the food classifications: raw foods, organic plant based whole foods, ethically sourced dairy, ethically sourced meat and fish, and processed, refined, unethical junk food.
6. **Breath Work:** For those who are comfortable in solitude, I recommend a daily twenty minutes breath work meditation. Breath is the physiological component we neglect the most, yet if harnessed properly it can be a tool for healing and rejuvenation. For beginners, I

suggest using a 4 x 4 seconds Box Breathing Technique (4 seconds in, 4 x hold, 4 x out, 4 x hold and repeat).

7. **Sound Healing:** Sound at the correct frequency can have remarkable healing effects. Sound healing works on the alignment of the vibrational frequency of the seven major chakras. Using chants or tuning forks, one can activate the properties of each chakra and unlock its healing potential.

Chakra	Frequency	Chant
1	396 Hz	Lam
2	417 Hz	Vam
3	528 Hz	Ram
4	639 Hz	Yam
5	741 Hz	Ham
6	852 Hz	Om
7	963 Hz	Om

8. **Take Up a New Challenge or Hobby:** One of the easiest ways to shift energy is to embrace transformation through change. Focusing on new tasks or challenges that draw your attention to yourself is a fantastic way to re-establish yourself as a priority in your own life.
9. **Journaling:** As an author, I am probably a little biased towards writing as a medium to practice introspection and achieve clarity. I have been journaling for close to twenty years and the one tip I have for you is that journaling works best if you approach it with purpose.

Set an intention, ask a question, and then attempt to dive deep into it using multiple lenses (perspectives).

10. **Solo Travel:** I have travelled to more than 120 countries (90 per cent of them solo). As someone who has been bitten hard by the travel bug, I can attest that nothing teaches you more about yourself than solo travel. Nothing forces you out of your comfort zone like solo travel. In a nutshell, it is your 'fast track' pass to inner healing, self-discovery, and personal growth.

Remember, your sense of self-worth is your fulcrum. It is what will allow you to restore balance and equilibrium in the most challenging moments of your life.

If you want to understand and cultivate a love for yourself:

1. Make a list of the five things you love the most. Are you a priority in your own life?
2. Define your core values
3. Self-examine the trauma and destructive patterns in your life
4. Acknowledge and accept the associated emotions and feelings
5. Forgive yourself and get ready to shift your energy and mindset
6. Energize and elevate your vibrational energy through cultivating healing routines and habits

TWO

Circles of Connection
(Relationships, Mind)

Write down the names of the five people closest to you. (Family and Friends)

1.

2.

3.

4.

5.

Before we come back to your answers, there is an odd phenomenon called the **Friendship Paradox**. It finds that *most people have fewer friends than their friends have, even though most people believe exactly the opposite to be true.*

It turns out that this paradox is in fact a statistical phenomenon which has to do with sampling bias. I bring it up because it segues into something more important: most of us are lonelier than we realize. In fact, in many societies, loneliness has reached epidemic proportions. Not only are we not mindful of our loneliness, we are not mindful of the quality of our support networks. Being more mindful of our relationships and more purposeful in cultivating quality relationships is the focus of this chapter. Its purpose is:

- To identify those people who are closest to you.
- To understand if these relationships are contributing to your growth.
- To evaluate the quality of these relationships.
- To interpret the science of friendships.
- To create a framework that allows you to enhance the quality of your relationships.

Going back to your answers, I would like you to remove the family members on your list for now. Why? As important and essential as family connections are, our commitment to them is often a matter of obligation and not choice. In large part, family is something we are born into. The focus of this chapter is on the relationships we choose. (We will deal with family dynamics separately.)

Now looking at the rest of your list, answer these few questions:

1. How many people do you have on your list?
2. How many of these individuals are your source of nourishment?
3. Do they add value to your life: financially, emotionally, spiritually or socially?
4. How many of them would you call when you are emotionally down?
5. On a scale of 1-10, how would you rate the quality of your interactions with them?

For most people, this first exercise is a moment of deep reflection. Many of you may have barely two names on the list when you remove family members; some may have only one. There is nothing wrong or unusual about this, but it can be unsettling to face the reality.

Moreover, the quality of those remaining relationships may be far from ideal. That truth is difficult to face as well, but awareness is the birthplace of transformation. Mindfully reflecting on the quality of the relationships in your life can give you the leverage to change the narrative in these relationships. Many of us are in relationships that deplete our emotional and spiritual energy banks. As I have mentioned previously, it is completely natural to have these types of relationships with family dependents. But outside of family, in those connections we purposefully choose, our relationships need to provide a base of nourishment, rejuvenation, and emotional and mental stability.

One Sunday evening, Katherine called me to chat about an unrelenting inner voice of self-criticism and sabotage. After a string of failed relationships, she was able to acknowledge that there was an underlying issue. Fears of abandonment and loneliness kept forcing her into patterns of clinginess, which often resulted in her driving her partners away. For the few who loved her enough to remain committed, she eventually questioned their intentions, doubted their love, and manifested a reason to leave.

I encouraged Katherine to think deeply about a single relationship with the following exercise.

The Equality Equation

Write down the name of the individual and nature of the relationship you have with him/her.

Now answer these four questions:

1. What am I giving to this relationship?
2. What am I receiving from this relationship?
3. What more would I like to give to this relationship?
4. What more would I like to receive from this relationship?

Without getting absorbed into the narrative or emotions of the relationship, I encouraged her to create a framework of her ideal relationship using these four questions. We can apply these four questions to any relationship. This reflective process will allow you to mindfully set your own terms for the relationship. From an arm's length, you will be able to determine if the relationship is a fair exchange of emotions, stability, security, and trust. Far too often, before evaluating each individual's contribution in a relationship, we get carried away by the emotions. At times, certain patterns may be a projection of some 'inner child' trauma; on the other hand, it is also possible that you are simply with a partner who is unresponsive or is attempting to sabotage the relationship. It is important that we accurately distinguish between the two. This exercise of framing the relationship is the perfect place to start.

We are often quick to call an individual a friend before we have established real trust. In doing so, we fail to grasp the full potential of a true friendship. In *Letters from a Stoic,* Seneca advised his colleagues to evaluate and judge before admitting someone as a friend. *'But when we finally do decide to call them friends, we must welcome them with heart and soul and speak unreservedly as you would with yourself.'*

Why do we fall into the trap of thinking so superficially about something as essential as friendship? Why do we confuse acquaintances with friends? We live in a world where, on social media like Facebook, we have more so-called 'friends' than we could possibly count. Yet, we are lonely.

Loneliness is a full-blown epidemic. According to the former surgeon general of the United States, loneliness shortens a lifespan in a way similar to smoking fifteen cigarettes a day. A recent meta-review of 70 studies showed that loneliness increases the risk of mortality by 26 per cent, even more than depression or anxiety.

More than simply an emotional state, loneliness affects us at the cellular level. Researchers have found that it switches on inflammation, while at the same time suppressing our natural immune response. As John Cacioppo, one of the world's leading experts on the topic, puts it, *'The level of toxicity from loneliness is stunning.'*

Clearly, we must make a more mindful and deliberate effort to cultivate human connections in our lives.

The Price of an Olympic Medal

Between 2007 and 2012, I was on the ATP Tour with many tennis professionals. As the sports scientist in charge, I was tasked with improving the physiology and psychology of my players. During this time, I had an intimate working relationship with the Indian Davis Cup players, Mahesh Bhupathi and Leander Peas. To say they were legends of the game would be an understatement. They amassed, between them, more than 100 ATP Tour titles, 30 Grand Slam titles, more than 1300 professional career wins, 181 Davis Cup representations and 12 Olympic Games appearances. Both players are recipients of the Padma Shri Award (India's highest civilian recognition) and to date they hold the record for the most consecutive Davis Cup wins in the history of the tournament.

At the 2008 Beijing Olympics, the quarter final match between Team India (Mahesh and Leander) and Team Switzerland (Roger Federer and Stanislas Wawrinka) was no contest to speak of. The Indians were dusted off in just over an hour. Unfortunately, no scorecard has a metric for team unity, but social science has taught us to read between the lines. In the lead up to Beijing, the constant friction between the two players was no secret and which is anything but conducive to optimal performance.

As author Jon Katzenbach puts it in his bestselling book *The Wisdom of Teams, 'Teams and good performance are inseparable. You cannot have one without the other.'*

Was it coincidental that the two teams that reached the final consisted of players who were not only great athletes, but who also had a healthy relationship on and off the court? When skills are at par, it is the quality of the relationships between players, coaches, friends, and family that can potentially tip the scales in one's favour. The question is, **what is the formula for a healthy relationship? And is it possible to fast-track trust in a relationship?**

Research does exist around the impact of cohesive relationships on performance. Erasmus University Rotterdam revealed that *team reflexivity* is a key factor in the effectiveness of a team. **Team reflexivity** is the extent to which teams reflect upon and modify their functioning. Reflexivity is the process through which teams learn from past failures and successes. It requires honest, effective communication, which is a by-product of a healthy relationship.

Are you able to communicate with your partner effectively enough to understand what is working and what isn't?

Relationships constitute one of the four domains in my Balance model. How we do or do not cultivate in our relationships is intimately connected to our core values, limiting beliefs, and overall harmony and happiness. In the ashram where I spent a few years living as a monk, I was constantly reminded of the importance of being associated with learned scholars and monks. The passage of knowledge that is deeply rooted in spirituality is known as lineage. It is through the cultivation of a relationship with such spiritually awakened individuals that we are able to absorb their teachings. Since relationships play such an integral role in our psyche and development, it is important that we understand the science of relationships.

Shasta Nelson is a Friendship Expert and author of *Frientimacy: How to Deepen Friendships for Lifelong Health and Happiness. 'A healthy friendship is about creating an environment through which both members can be seen in a satisfying way,'* she states. Her research on friendship, loneliness, and relationships led her to identify three key variables that contribute to such an environment – variables she terms it as a **Friendship Triangle.**

P + C + V = Healthy Relationship

P = Positivity
C = Consistency
V = Vulnerability

1. **Positivity:** No one wants to befriend someone who is always negative, complaining, and depressed.

Think about the type of energy you prefer to have around you. Relationships that are light and have accompanying feelings of happiness, gratitude, joy, bliss, and contentment are not only enjoyable but rejuvenating as well. *'This does not prevent friends from venting,'* Nelson says. *'But we need to be mindful that to maintain the balance, we need five positive interactions for every negative one.'*

2. **Consistency:** Isn't making friends at work or school easy? According to a Workplace Options survey, 85 per cent of individuals between 18 and 29 are likely to be in a relationship with a co-worker, and 31 per cent of them go on to get married. The science behind this is consistency. The more we interact with someone, the stronger the bond gets. Go back to your list of the closest people to you. How often do you interact with them? Probably a chicken and egg situation. Are they close to you because you interact with them, or do you interact with them because they are close to you? Irrespective, research highlights the connection between consistency and trust in a relationship.
3. **Vulnerability:** The secret to emotional connection is intimacy and the pathway to intimacy is vulnerability. By sharing our struggles as well as intimate positive experiences, we deepen our emotional connection with people. Dr Brené Brown describes vulnerability as, *'The birthplace of love, belonging, joy, courage, empathy, and creativity. It is the source of hope, empathy, accountability and authenticity.'* In her new book *Daring Greatly*, she

says, *'Being vulnerable and open is mutual and an integral part of the trust building process.'*

In an attempt to test Nelson's friendship equation, I randomly picked ten people whom I had met at some stage in my life but had not been in touch with for many years. I initiated contact with a few positive, light messages, wishing them well and sending them love. I maintained the consistency of these messages for a few weeks. After some time, I suggested that we meet in person. Within a week, I had met all ten individuals. Each interaction was powerful and inspiring in its own way. After a month of consistent, positive contact, I felt ready to deepen these connections. As I did so, I tried to be mindful of the three variables Nelson suggests are keys to a healthy friendship. I was conscious of being intimate and vulnerable while maintaining positivity to keep the energy from becoming too heavy. Yet I also allowed myself to share difficult feelings. The experience confirmed Nelson's assertion that the variables – **Positivity, Consistency, and Vulnerability – are indeed like the three legs of a stool, helping in keeping a relationship stable and well-balanced.**

I also observed the importance of reciprocity and familiarity. When I shared something with one of my renewed connections, each individual reciprocated with a story that matched my emotional state. I found this quite fascinating. Reciprocity was automatic and reflexive, and the emotion each person chose to reciprocate with matched the emotion of my sharing. There is actually a science to this. It is called the **familiarity–attraction link,** which states that the higher the degree of familiarity in the information we share, the deeper the connection. The ancient Greeks called this *homophily*, which is the tendency to associate or bond with someone who is like you. It turns out that emotionally exposing yourself comes with risk, but the reward is deeper, more meaningful connections, provided there is familiarity in the reciprocity.

In the chapter on 'Self-love' I quoted Aristotle as saying: *'True friendship is possible only between virtuous people, and so only between people whose natures are formed.'*

Let's take this concept forward:

Think back to an altercation or argument you may have had with a friend. When you begin to examine the underlying cause, you will likely notice that the reason for the argument was a misalignment in a core belief or virtue. One party acted in a manner which was not in alignment with the core values that held their relationship together.

Virtue comes from Latin word *virtus* and the Greek word *arete* which refers to moral excellence. A virtue is a quality that is deemed morally good and forms the foundation of a strong bond or relationship. Irrespective of the situation, (arguments with a partner, lover, co-founder, friends, business colleagues) all interpersonal conflicts are born of a breach of a core value.

Virtues are such an integral part of our growth and development. They have been spoken about since time immemorial. **Christianity** focuses on four cardinal virtues: *temperance, prudence, courage,* and *justice*. **Bushido**, the samurai way of life, is characterized by eight main virtues: *righteousness, heroic courage, compassion, respect,* *honesty, honour, duty* and *self-control*. **Buddhism's** four *brahmavihara* (divine states) regarded as virtues, are: *metta* (loving-kindness), *karuna* (compassion), *mudita* (altruism) and *upeksha* (equanimity). **Daoism** describes virtue (*de*) as personal character, inner strength and integrity. In **Hinduism**, a moral, ethical, virtuous life is characterized by the word dharma. Scriptures describe ten virtues necessary for a dharmic life: *dhriti* (courage), *kshama* (forgiveness), *dama* (temperance), *asteya* (non-covetousness), *saucha* (inner purity), *indriyani-graha* (control of one's senses), *dhi* (reflective prudence), *vidya* (wisdom), *satyam* (truthfulness), and *akrodha* (freedom from anger). Running parallel to Hinduism, **Jainism** lays down five virtues needed for enlightenment: *ahimsa* (non-violence), *satya* (truthfulness), *asteya* (non-stealing), *aparigraha* (non-attachment) and *brahmacharya* (celibacy). In **Islam**, the Quran which is believed to be the word of God is said to highlight three virtues: *fadl* (bounty), *taqwa* (piety) and *salah* (righteousness).

In 2004, Martin Seligman and Christopher Peterson concluded a three-year study that identified 24 traits that were categorized into six broad virtues that exhibited a *'surprising amount of similarity across cultures and strongly indicat[ed] a historical and cross-cultural convergence.'* The six virtues were **courage, justice, humanity, temperance, transcendence** and **wisdom**.

The seven cultures mentioned above (Christianity, Bushido, Buddhism, Daoism, Hinduism, Jainism, Islam) form the major part of the world's belief systems. If these were the values that were indoctrinated into our consciousness, aligning with them would be part of our subconscious programming. It therefore stands to reason that any misalignment from these core values or virtues would likely cause an altercation or rift.

Understanding the virtues that resonate strongest with you is not just the cornerstone of a healthy relationship with oneself, but is also pivotal in every healthy relationship. As Nelson and Brown have pointed out, intimacy that is born from vulnerability can deepen connections, provided that the sharing is in alignment with your core values. Intimate sharing that breaches one's innate core value system could potentially cause the end of any relationship.

Let's try a reflective thought exercise:

1. Write down your initial list of names. (From the opening question in this chapter)
2. Write down the core values that define you. (From 'Self-love')
3. Try to identify three core values in each person you have on the list.
4. Look for the similarities between what defines you and what you see in others.

List of Friends	Your Core Values (CV)

Friend 1: 3 × CV	Friend 2: 3 × CV	Friend 3: 3 × CV

Most of these relationships hinge on a set of core values or virtues that resonate with both parties. If the intimacy complements these values, the emotional connectivity will become stronger. If any party breaches these virtues, the relationship could potentially be threatened. Most relationships are strong enough to withstand conflicts. What they cannot survive is a lack of security. A breach in a core value can erode the safety and security upon which the relationship has been built. This does not mean every breach is the end of a relationship. Remember, we have the *Forgiveness Window of Opportunity*, which means if we put our egos aside, we can find a viable solution and save the relationship.

The Friendship Equation highlights one simple point. **Quality friendships require time, effort, love, and intimacy**. Given our current lifestyles, I wonder if it is possible to dedicate the necessary amount of time and effort to cultivate more than four or five meaningful relationships.

Aristotle believed it is wise to not have too many friends. *'Every friendship takes time and having too many friends means less time and energy to give to each friend. Therefore, a man with many friends will have many shallow friendships, but a man of few companions will have the richer relationships.'*

Borrowing from the wisdom of the Greeks, I created the **Concentric Circles of Friendships**.

This is a three-tiered system that helps you differentiate between friends and acquaintances. In creating this thought exercise, I realized that the English language does not allow us to accurately distinguish between the various relationships in our lives. Seneca was right. *We use the word 'friend' too loosely, but the problem is that we do not have an adequate term to describe an individual who is more than an acquaintance but isn't quite in your inner circle just yet.*

Let's try this exercise:

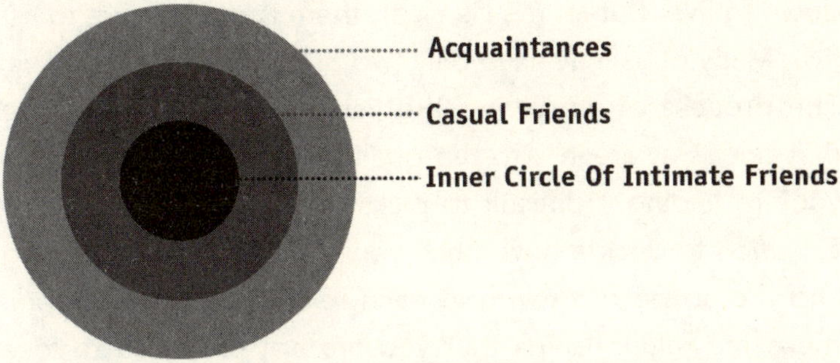

Inner Circles of Intimate Friends

This category might include as many as four or five individuals – in some cases more. Then again, it is perfectly fine to have even one or two. It is not a contest, and this is an area of our lives where quality definitely outweighs quantity.

The University of Oxford anthropologist Robin Dunbar studied the relationship between brain size and social relationships in an effort to determine how many people a human brain can accommodate in its social circle. Dunbar's research[1] showed that the deepest level of connectivity can accommodate only five individuals. This means, according to social and behavioural sciences, you can truly do justice to five intimate, meaningful connections.

For me, these are the (at most) five relationships outside your family relationships that you are deeply invested in. It is a reciprocal relationship of love, emotional intimacy, support, and stability.

I started by listing everyone I thought might belong in this group; then, through introspection, I narrowed the list down to five. But let me be clear: there is no pressure to list five. Many of us may have only two or three intimate friends. The process of narrowing the list is a powerful exercise that brings awareness to the quality of each relationship. If you are finding it difficult to pick, you can use the *Equality Equation* to decide how much you are giving and receiving and the scope of growth in each relationship. Remember, these are relationships that you are not prepared to lose under any circumstances.

Casual Friendships

Based on Dunbar's ratio of neocortical volume to brain volume formulae, the second layer of friendships can accommodate ten individuals. This level is rather interesting. It consists of friends, colleagues, mentors, or business partners who add value to your life and vice versa, but the connections rarely result in deep, intimate sharing. Personally, this level has contributed to my biggest growth curve as this second tier is filled with mentors and work colleagues who challenge me on a daily basis. These are often the friendships that challenge you to become the best version of yourself.

On a related note, in his book *Give and Take*, Adam Grant explores why connections in our second (and sometimes third) circles can be so powerful. In the language of networking, he refers to these connections as 'weak' or 'dormant' ties. Precisely because you may not be in regular contact with people in your second or third circle, they are more likely to give you surprising or unexpected insights.

Acquaintances

While Dunbar has created four individual tiers, I prefer to restrict my grouping to three levels. Everyone beyond the 15-20 friends in the first two tiers is just an acquaintance. An acquaintance could be someone you have just met or someone you have known for a while. These levels are not linked to the amount of time you have known someone but rather the amount (and quality) of time you spend with them. If your encounters are random, and the degree of interaction very surface-level, this individual can be most likely classified as an acquaintance. Again, the standard is one of quality, not quantity.

The Concentric Circles of Friendships is an exercise in introspection and honesty. In my own case, I realized that *I resist calling someone an acquaintance; perhaps I found the designation dismissive of someone I truly value. So by default I thought of them as friends – yet in doing so, I moved all my relationships into a wide grey area, instead of having clarity on what each relationship meant to me.*

This isn't just a classification exercise. It is a healing exercise. It requires clarity of thought, courage, and honesty – and eventually, transparency. When you find the courage to group your relationships into these three tiers, you will see more clearly what is required to maintain those relationships.

In the chapters to come, I will introduce you to the concept of switching lenses. Till then, here is a lens through which you could view this perspective.

Why would I invest in being your friend if you cannot find the courage to acknowledge my role in your life?

I have spent the better part of my adult life travelling the world with professional athletes. When you spend this much time with anyone, they can easily and automatically fall within your 'Inner Circle of Intimate Friends'. As the person charged with pushing them beyond their limits, I had to consciously manage this situation. I needed to be close enough to get them to share their deep emotional insecurities, and that involved a certain degree of intimacy; but at no point could I let it cloud my judgment.

In individual sports it is easier to manage this intricate balance. In team sports, it is trickier when an athlete's emotional state has the potential to impact the performance of the team.

During a professional assignment with a cricket team in Caribbean Premier League, I had a cricketer who was emotionally conflicted. He walked around as though he had a mountain of burdens on his shoulders. When I eventually got a chance to speak to him, I realized that it had nothing to do with his performance. Despite being an extremely successful cricketer, he was in deep financial trouble. On the surface this just did not make sense. When I probed him further, he revealed that he was surrounded by family and so-called 'friends' who were always expecting him to provide for them financially. None of them had jobs, but their lifestyle was filled with extravagance.

This is an example of how a lack of clearly defined boundaries in friendships can be emotionally taxing on one's time and resources.

In this situation, you can play the victim card, or you can realize you have the power to change this narrative.

> **Realization #5**
>
> *You have to see yourself as a co-creator of your destiny.*

In his book *The Four Loves*, C. S. Lewis says, '*Not everyone will experience romantic love, but everyone can gain a friend.*' Such is the power of a true bond built on strong virtues and morals.

Lewis succinctly articulates that everyone can gain a friend, but the truth is not all friendships are equal. The most distinguishable differences in friendship often come down to gender differences. We have all perceived these differences in our relationships with various gender types; however, I was interested in understanding the neuroscientific reasoning behind this. To explain this, scientists have studied four areas with respect to the male and female brain: processing, chemistry, structure, and activity.

Processing: The male brain utilizes seven times more grey matter, while the female brain utilizes ten times more white matter. The result is that men have more tunnel-vision and can be highly-focused on tasks while females are better able to transition between tasks, making them quantifiably more adept at multi-tasking.

Chemistry: While both brains process neurochemicals, they do so in varying degrees. One such difference is that males less oxytocin (the chemical responsible for bonding, social recognition, and group memories) than females.

Structure: Females brains have a larger hippocampus (emotional and memory centre) and a higher density of neural connections. As a result, females are able to input and absorb more sensorial and emotive information than males.

Activity: The female brain has a higher degree of blood flow, particularly in an area called the *cingulate gyrus,* which causes females to ruminate on and revisit emotional memories more than a male brain. Males tend to reflect only briefly on an emotive memory, analyze it, and then move onto another task. Sometimes the other task is completely unrelated to that feeling, thus creating a false perception that males avoid their feelings.

Scientists have discovered hundreds of neurological differences between the male and female brain that explain the subtle nuances in how each gender forms meaningful relationships and bonds. Knowing how to account for these differences is an essential element in your pursuit for balance.

Emotional healing is tough. It is a combination of many elements that I described in the SAFE Method (Self Examination, Acknowledge and Accept, Forgiveness, Energize and Elevate). SAFE is a process that requires time, space, and positive energy in order to translate it into real action and change. It took me a long time to fully absorb the roles each gender can play in one's healing journey.

Men, by the sheer nature of how their brain functions, are hard-wired to be rational and solution-driven. You would have noticed that when you try venting to a male counterpart, they are (not always, but often) ready to offer a solution to the problem even before you finish speaking. This is a generalization; but, more often than not, men struggle to be emotionally present for a prolonged period of time.

Females, on the other hand, are exceptional at holding space and energy for a friend as they take time to understand, acknowledge, accept, forgive, and heal. Because the female brain is hard-wired to revisit sensorial and emotive information, they have the capacity to be present in a specific emotional state for longer periods of time. In a nutshell, the female brain isn't always in a hurry to find a solution.

Healing requires a balance of both the feminine and the masculine energies. The two energies cannot entirely be reduced to gender, as both men and women possess different combinations of masculine and feminine energy. Either way, we need to be mindful of incorporating both into our lives. We need relationships with people who are compassionate enough to hold space, time, and energy for you. Yet, we also require friends who can lift the smoke screen and help us find clarity through an actionable solution. Neither process can be rushed, but both are essential. As you ponder all of this, I encourage you to find your perfect gender balance in the first two tiers of your Concentric Circles of Friendship.

The Fundamental Principles of Conflict

In 1976, psychotherapist Dr Lester Luborsky was busy reading transcripts of psychotherapy sessions when he discovered a pattern within the conversations between clinicians and their patients. He was able to identify **three core elements to every conflict:**

1. Each individual in a conflict wants to be **understood, empathized with,** and **seen.**
2. Each individual wants to be **respected, valued,** and **treated fairly.**
3. Each individual wants to feel good about themselves.

Relationships that are devoid of conflict are few and far between. In fact, conflict gets a bad 'rep' despite the irony that we learn the most about ourselves and others through conflict. Such is the paradox of life. We despise pain and conflict, yet it is through such struggles that we evolve and mature.

In our quest to deepen the intimacy in our relationships, we may for innumerable reasons reach a point of conflict. If we are mindful that in every conflict the person just wants to be understood and seen, respected and treated fairly, and feel good about the outcome, the conflict can lead to a deeper, more meaningful relationship – rather than to an abrupt end to something that could have blossomed.

This is yet another example of how growth requires that we step out of (or be pushed out of) our comfort zone. It also illustrates our earlier distinction between static and dynamic balance. Conflict may make us feel out-of-balance, and we may therefore try to avoid or repress that conflict in order to restore balance. Yet the static balance of a conflict-free life is rarely attainable, or desirable. In fact, real harmony and balance come from staying with conflict and discomfort and allowing it to teach us. As you explore the questions raised in this chapter, you may feel tested, challenged, and uncomfortable. You may feel pushed off your emotional centre. If you follow the process through, however, you will return to a deeper balance. The struggle will be worth it.

If you want to cultivate happier, healthier, more intimate relationships:

1. Make a list of the five friends closest to you
2. Evaluate each relationship using the equality equation
3. Understand how you can deepen each connection with the friendship equation
4. Align your core values with each relationship
5. Create your concentric circles of friendship
6. Evaluate the gender balance
7. Be mindful of the fundamental principles of conflict

THREE

Start with Your Strengths (Mind and Body)

Athletic performance is all about learning to leverage your strengths. Helping elite athletes do so has been my primary focus for the last twenty years.

There has been a lot written in recent times about the development and utilization of one's strengths. What else can I contribute to this topic?

When you spend over two decades working with professional athletes and every minute of your day is dedicated to analyzing and improving their performance, you develop the precision and clarity needed to identify and cultivate a strength. Everything you do is viewed through the lens of performance enhancement.

This chapter is my story from inside the locker room. It grows out of twenty years of working with and watching the best sportspeople practice, compete, recover, and rejuvenate. I was the one who pushed my athletes beyond every conceivable barrier – physiological and psychological. I helped redefine their upper limits. At times, those limits were the upper limits of human potential.

I had to make the uncomfortable comfortable.
I had to make the unfamiliar familiar.
I had to make the impossible possible.
This is what it takes to win.

Through the anecdotes and exercises in this chapter, we will create a paradigm shift – one that makes you realize that everything you desire is just outside your comfort zone. I will give you the key to the door that unlocks that space. There you will learn how pushing beyond your limits is the key to finding balance.

As we discussed previously, the balance we are aiming for is dynamic, not static. Dynamic balance is not a comfortable midpoint or a soothing symmetry. Pushing your limits and going outside your comfort zone involves creating a momentary imbalance in the pursuit of a deeper balance in the long run.

In this chapter, we will discover:

- The definition of strength
- The anatomy of strength
- How to know your strength
- Techniques to develop your strength
- Achieving flow

In the world of performance sport, the word 'strength' is not used loosely. In the sacred sanctum of the locker-room, when athletes, coaches, and support staff talk about the strength of an opposition, you can be assured that the skill in question could potentially turn a game in one second. Athletes have mastered that skill and studied every conceivable angle from which to utilize it, all in the pursuit of gaining an advantage. Sometimes that advantage is razor thin; at other times it is formidable.

The Definition of Strength

When an athlete identifies a skill as a strength, it has to be a skill that could give them a competitive advantage in a high stakes environment. If they cannot see that skill winning them a game, getting them out of a specific situation, or helping them shift the advantage in their favour, it is not a strength. This is the difference between an amateur athlete and a professional. A professional has an acute understanding of his strengths and is therefore in a position to leverage them.

In sport, it is easy to identify the technical strengths of an individual. Athletes typically strategize their entire game plan around that skill. It is that skill that gives them a competitive advantage in a high pressure environment. Yet, having worked with thousands of athletes – professional and amateur – it has become evident that a pure technical competency may not necessarily be the secret to success. There is no denying that technical competence (skill) is a vital ingredient; but in the world of high-pressure sport, to get to the top 1 per cent you need to understand and develop other aspects of your personality and temperament that drive performance.

Over the years, there have been a number of tools developed to help you understand your strengths. I have personally tested most of them before applying them to the athletes and corporate executives I work with. Identifying strengths in an unbiased manner is the difference between winning and losing, gold and silver, and the world knowing who you are and fading into irrelevance. These are the stakes in an environment where the margin for error is miniscule and the penalty for failure high.

Can you remember who won the 100 metre finals at the London Olympic Games in 2012?

Most people know it was Usain Bolt.

Can you remember who came in second? Hardly anyone will ever know that it was Yohan Blake, who finished with a personal best of 9.75 seconds, just 12/100th of a second slower than Bolt's Olympic Record of 9.63 seconds. That's a fraction longer than the speed of the blink of an eye, yet for the person who finished second, it is an eternity. It is all that stood between Yohan and the world knowing who he is.

This is all well and good, if you understand what your strengths are. However, most people do not know what are these unique set of skills they possess.

> *'Most do not know what their strengths are. When you ask them, they look at you with a blank stare, or they respond in terms of subject knowledge, which is the wrong answer.'* – Peter Drucker

Dr Donald Clifton, the Father of Strength Psychology, conducted a study of 1.1 million people across 63 countries. He asked them one question, **'What do you think will help**

you improve more: knowing your strengths or knowing your weaknesses?'

The results were amazing. Most individuals wanted to know their weaknesses, assuming that this knowledge would give them the opportunity to improve and, hence, succeed.

However, there was a small subset of people interested in knowing their strengths. These individuals were, it just so happens, also the most successful across the sample population. The performers in the world are focused on knowing their strengths.

This fact was confirmed by a 2002 Corporate Leadership Council study of more than 19,000 employees across 29 countries. The results were mind-blowing. When individuals focused on their strengths, their performance improved by 36.4 per cent. In contrast, emphasis on weaknesses produced a 26.8 per cent decline in performance.

There is now a consensus in a number of fields – including sports, business, and positive psychology – that the most effective approach to developing yourself (or others) is to identify existing strengths and use those strengths as a foundation for further growth.

The Anatomy of a Strength

Dr Clifton opens his book *Now, Discover Your Strengths* with a warning against focusing on weaknesses. *'Guided by the belief that good is the opposite of bad, mankind has for centuries pursued its fixation with fault and failing. Faults and failings deserve study, but they reveal little about strengths. Strengths have their own patterns.'*

As his survey suggested, the most successful among us focus on strengths instead. *'What great leaders have in common is that each truly knows his or her strengths – and can call on the right strength at the right time.'*

Which begs the question: What exactly is strength? Are our strengths innate, or do we acquire them?

Clifton breaks down strengths into three components:

- **Talent:** an innate, natural ability or aptitude
- **Knowledge:** the theoretical or practical understanding of a subject
- **Skill:** a proficiency developed through training or experience

We convert an innate talent into strength by acquiring knowledge and skill.

STRENGTH = TALENT + KNOWLEDGE + SKILL

One essential thing to understand is that talents may evolve, but they don't change. So the Clifton StrengthFinder is really a TalentFinder. Once we identify our innate talents, we can then go about acquiring the knowledge and skills that complement those talents. The mistake many make is to go off in search of knowledge and skills without first understanding their innate talents.

Knowing the anatomy of a strength is one thing. But what about the process of converting talents into strengths? In my own experience cultivating strengths in everyone from high-performing athletes to CEOs, I have found that this process must be marked by the following four qualities:

1. **Consistency:** The strength should be executed with efficiency, proficiency and replicability.

2. **Successful:** The strength needs to gain you a competitive advantage in any environment.
3. **Enjoyment:** The process of executing the strength should be fun, enjoyable, and with ease.

As Dr Clifton says, the acid test of strength is if you can see yourself doing it *repeatedly, happily, and successfully.* After spending two decades with professional athletes, I have identified one more key variable in strength-building.

4. **Coachability:** An individual's willingness to learn and embrace change.

Success in the world of sport can be fleeting. The only way to ring fence your success is to be willing to change what is already working.

During the 2003 Cricket World Cup in South Africa, I was the appointed Technical Analyst of the Indian cricket team. Our match at Kingsmead cricket ground was against a formidable English opposition. The Kingsmead pitch traditionally bounced a lot more than normal, which enticed fast bowlers to pitch the ball shorter. In our preparation for this match, we had to anticipate and prepare for two things:

- The tall, lanky English bowlers were going to try to rattle our batters with short-pitched deliveries sliding into the body.
- Our best chance of bowling England out was to get wickets early by utilizing the moisture in the pitch and wind to swing the ball.

This required our players to change an approach that had won us three consecutive games.

The Indian batsmen changed their batting stance to increase their stability base, while the Indian bowlers practiced fuller lengths deliveries. Both of these were completely unnatural for the players. However, their willingness to change what was working resulted in an emphatic victory by 83 runs.

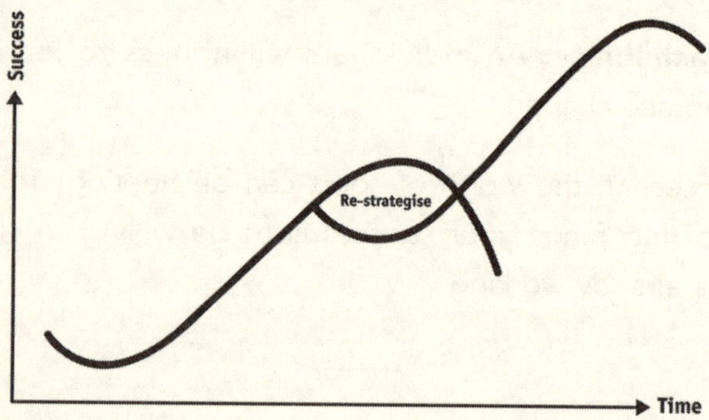

The strategy of always looking to improve when you are already 'on top of your game' is known as the Sigmoid Curve[1]. The curve is a growth model composed of three phases: **the learning phase**, **the growth phase**, and **the decline phase**. The curve depicts slow growth in the learning phase, followed by rapid growth in phase two, and then a decline in phase three. In phase one, you gather knowledge, and in phase two, you implement that knowledge. The decline of phase three reflects the fact that all information and knowledge has a 'half-life' – and that's what works today won't necessarily work tomorrow. In other words, it is a scientific affirmation of the principle of impermanence.

The practical implication is that the only way to keep evolving and growing is to start a new growth curve before the current one peaks and goes into decline. Even when things are going well, we must plan again, reinvent, and restrategize. This is what the best athletes, corporate executives, and leaders in the world do.

Realization #6

Your willingness to change what is working could become your greatest strength.

How to Know Your Strength

Clifton's StrengthFinder is a tool that presents you with pairs of statements, captures your choices, sorts them, and reflects back on your most dominant patterns of behaviour, thereby highlighting your greatest potential for *real* strength. This tool is now widely used in the business world, in counselling, and in education.[2]

This is an excellent place to start your journey of self-reflection and self-assessment. The innate talents you identify are drawn from thirty-four 'themes' that fall into four broad domains: Strategic Thinking, Relationship Building, Influencing, and Executing.

Strategic Thinking	Relationship Building	Influencing	Executing
Analytical	Adaptability	Activator	Achiever
Context	Connectedness	Command	Arranger

Futuristic	Developer	Communication	Belief
Ideation	Empathy	Competition	Consistency
Input	Harmony	Maximizer	Deliberative
Intellection	Includer	Self-assurance	Discipline
Learner	Individualization	Significance	Focus
Strategic	Positivity	Woo	Responsibility
	Relator		Restorative

Note: We will use the results of your assessment as we progress.

Just as important as understanding a strength is knowing when to use it. In the book *The Science of Hitting*, Ted Williams (a professional baseball player who hit more than 300 home runs) created his 'Three Rules to Hit By'. The first rule was **to get a good ball to hit**.

Ted mapped his swing zone at the batting plate. He was able to quantify his probability of hitting a home run based on his 'sweet spot' – the area of the pitch map that he knew gave him the highest probability of success. According to Williams, **having the perfect swing is useless if you don't know which ball to swing at**. When you understand your strength, you have to have the patience to wait for an opportunity to use it.

Warren Buffett frequently mentions Williams' theory of hitting. *'If he waited for the pitch that was really in his sweet spot, he would bat .400,'* Buffett says. *'If he had to swing at something on the lower corner, he would probably bat .235,'* Buffett says he takes the same approach to investing. *'The trick in investing is just to sit there and watch pitch after pitch go by and wait for the one right in your sweet spot.'*

Every aspect of this book is part of an inner journey of self-reflection. A gentle process that allows you to reflect on the physical, emotional, spiritual, and psychological aspects of your life. Through reflection, you honour your spirit. Remember, the most important promise you can make to yourself is this commitment that allows your spirit to soar beyond every conceivable limit.

In the previous chapters, we attempted to define the self and your relationships. Here, we have begun to scratch below the surface in order to unlock your potential. When you operate from a position of strength, you allow your soul to flourish. Fear will melt away, your self-esteem and consciousness will rise, and you will welcome the power of abundance into your life. You will, for the first time perhaps, feel truly alive.

This paragraph is a gentle reminder to be fearless in the quest to find your true self. Search within the depths of your soul. Forget what was. Look to the future with gusto, knowing that the world is going to experience the best version of yourself and nothing less. This is the only way to truly honour your spirit.

Step one to understand your strengths was the online StrengthFinder assessment. I use this tool to help individuals differentiate between a skill and a strength. A talent becomes a strength when you begin to understand the nuances of how it functions and how best to leverage it.

- The deeper your understanding, the stronger the strength.

- The stronger the strength, the simpler the explanation.
- The simpler the explanation, the greater the learning.

In other words, **the curve of strength development takes us from simplicity to complexity and back to simplicity.** As we deepen our understanding of any subject matter, or of ourselves, we initially move from a simplistic view to a more sophisticated one. Yet genius and insight ultimately lie in a radical simplicity in which we strip away what is unnecessary, like a sculptor chiseling away at a piece of granite until only the essential form remains.

> *'The ability to simplify means to eliminate the unnecessary so that the necessary may speak.'* – Hans Hofmann

Let us now introspect through a series of questions:

Be as thorough as possible in answering each of these questions. This is where we begin to interpret your thoughts, feelings, and ideas.

1. Which aspect of your work you love the most?
2. What are the core skills that you execute with ease?
3. Which aspect of your work brings the most comfort and joy to others?
4. What is the most rewarding feeling you give to others?
5. What are you the proudest of?
6. What is your most unique talent?
7. What do you really enjoy doing?
8. What do you get complimented the most for?

By answering these questions, you will find commonality in two areas:

- what makes you happy, and,
- what has the biggest impact on others.

True strengths meet at the confluence of your personal happiness and the impact you have on others. When you function from this space, you embody self-transcendence and live a life of fulfillment.

The Multiple Lenses of Strength

The Tour De France is the biggest cycling event of the year, and for 110 years, no British cyclist had ever won the event. British cycling has been facing its toughest challenge to date. To change the fate of the organization, they brought in Dave Brailsford as the Director of Performance. This former professional cyclist was adamant that the theory of marginal gains would help them rewrite history. Perhaps it did. At the Beijing Olympics, the team won seven out of the ten available gold medals in track cycling. They then repeated this extraordinary feat at the London Olympics in 2012. Under Dave, the British cycling team won three out of four Tour De France events in the recent past. Brailsford describes his approach as follows: *'The whole principle came from the idea that if you broke down everything you could think of that goes into riding a bike, and then improve it by 1 per cent, you will get a significant increase when you put them all together.'*

This theory of marginal gains is the foundation of sports science. Every performance director or sports scientist looks for those incremental gains that could contribute to a competitive advantage in a game. It is what we do every second of every day. As someone who has spent a lifetime working with professional athletes, I can honestly tell you that getting a 1 per cent performance gain from any single variable consistently at the cutting edge of the sport is easier said than done.

While the theory of marginal gains cannot always guarantee success, it does do something equally powerful. **It shifts the magnifying glass to every possible facet of performance.**

There are five areas in which you could have strengths:

- Physiological (Body)
- Technical (Skill)
- Emotional (Resilience)
- Psychological (Mind)
- Social (Connect)

I work with professional athletes, corporate executives, and terminally ill patients. At times, a technical strength cannot help heal an illness; or a physiological strength cannot help with the anxiety of 'big point' nerves. This got me thinking.

If a strength can give you a significant advantage, why not look for the strengths in every aspect of your wellbeing. This realization sent me down a wonderfully exciting rabbit hole.

For each component of an individual's wellbeing, I started to map their strengths through scientifically validated tests. Each strength then layered upon another to eventually help me create the perfect blueprint for the optimization of human potential. I used gene mapping to design physical training programmes, gut microbiome tests to study, understand,

and reculture gut bacteria, food allergies and intolerances to design dietary guidelines that prevented inflammation and controlled glycemic variability, 3D biomechanical analysis to map high risk muscular skeletal injuries, dermatoglyphics assessments to learn about the processing strength of every cortex of their brain, and psycho-geometric and emotional social competency tests to deep dive into the personality of the individual.

Blood pathology markers, voice markers, sleep markers, gene markers and hundreds more. The goal was to find the untapped potential within every individual component and then do everything I possibly could to leverage it. The results were remarkable. From winning Olympic medals to reversing cancer, suddenly anything was possible.

So, what does this mean for you? It is not realistic for the average person to do such an exhaustive inventory of strengths.

In his book *Atomic Habits,* James Clear offers a more practical approach. *'Out of all the possible actions we could take, the one that is realized is the one that delivers the most value for the least effort. We are motivated to do what is easy.'* In my own life, I attempt to do as thorough a survey of my strengths as is possible. But when it comes to taking action, I try to identify the one area where a change will yield the greatest results.

Similarly, for my clients, I create roadmaps that allow them to build habits that are easy to execute and successful. You too can do the same. Throughout the book, I suggest a few online tests and some physiological ones as well. Take these tests. Understand yourself. Build habits that leverage your strengths. You will start to see amazing results and the sense of ease that accompanies your new found success. It will motivate you to keep going. Nothing motivates us like success. I have seen exceptionally talented individuals achieve nothing, while others who aren't so genetically gifted succeed through hard work. The difference between a champion and you is that champions know their strengths and do everything in their power to capitalize on them. Armed with knowledge, you can do the same.

Ask Your Friends

The StrengthFinder assessment and the introspective questions were both self-exploratory techniques to understand your strengths. After completing both of these exercises, you will start to notice a few similarities in the answers. You can cross reference the common answers from your introspective questions against the StrengthFinders traits. This will give you a deeper understanding of your innate strengths.

You are then ready to incorporate insight and feedback from others. As the founder and CEO of a healthcare startup, I would always encourage my leadership team to conduct an anonymous exercise to get an unbiased opinion of their respective strengths. I would ask them to write an email to ten people (friends, family, colleagues, co-workers, fellow entrepreneurs, mentors and partners) and request them to answer these questions:

- What are your five greatest strengths? (Elaborate as much as possible)

- How energized do they feel when they interact with you? (Rate on a scale of 1-10)
- What is the emotion you invoke in them?
- What in their opinion is your greatest achievement?
- If you were not doing your current job, what is the one career option they think you would be successful at?

It is important to make your list of people as diverse as possible. In your attempt to get meaningful and articulated answers, you may have to go back and forth over email to ensure that each question is answered in depth. This exercise is an excellent way to get an external perspective. Search for similarities in the answers. Once again, you will notice certain key words surface. Match these key strengths to your self-exploratory answers.

What is the degree of similarity between these answers? **Is your perception of your strengths in alignment with how others perceive you?**

Monk-like Discipline

There is a saying. Practice makes you perfect. It sounds correct, but it isn't.

Perfect practice makes you perfect. This is the mantra in the world of mastery.

There are two components to mastering a strength:

- the first is the discipline needed to learn that skill, and
- the consistency of practicing it daily.

Let me explain.

This was a lesson I learnt from my life as a monk. When I moved into the ashram, one of the rituals we had to abide by was the practice of waking up at 3 a.m. for morning meditation. To wake up at 3 a.m., you have to be in bed no later than 9 p.m. While I was happy to be in the ashram, I struggled to let go of my old habits. Habits that kept me connected to my old life. One of those habits was sleeping late. For the first two months, I hardly got any rest. I would fall asleep at midnight and in a few hours, I was woken up for meditation.

I remember sitting in the meditation room with my head covered, struggling to keep the eyes open. How could I focus on my meditation if I had barely got any rest?

This internal battle between my old life and the new one consumed me for months. It took me almost six months to fully accept my life as a monk. As I explained earlier, growth requires that we step out of our comfort zone, and when we do so, we feel a momentary imbalance (one that in my case lasted six months) until we are able to establish a new balance, a new equilibrium. We have to become comfortable with this ebb and flow and not expect an unchanging balance.

The moment I made this decision to fully accept my new life, the inner voice that kept distracting me suddenly disappeared. A negative habit will consume you right up until that moment you abandon it. I was now able to sleep by 9 p.m., wake up fresh at 3 a.m., and focus on the task at hand. From that moment on, my meditation practice began to deepen. Month by month, I was able to feel the power of focused meditation. From a new clarity of thought and being able to absorb knowledge from the universe, to being able to raise my vibrational energy. Each rising sun brought with it a new gift.

Why am I saying this to you? This isn't a lesson on the importance of meditation. It is a lesson on discipline. **Discipline is sticking to something long enough for it to break you before it makes you.** I have read many books and quotes about the time needed to cultivate a habit. Some said thirty days and others said ninety. For me, as long as you have a fixed time frame in mind, you can motivate yourself to push towards it. *When you stick to a process for longer than any and every conceivable time frame you have in your mind, that is the discipline it takes to become a master.*

Before I decided to move into the ashram, I was a High Performance Coach with a state cricket team – the Kwa Zulu Natal Dolphins. Back then, they were a formidable force in the South African domestic cricket system. One of our stalwart players was the legendary batsman Jonty Rhodes, whose reputation as the greatest fielder in the game soon surpassed every batting accolade he achieved.

Jonty's commitment to excellence was like nothing I had ever seen before. Every single day, when the team practice was over, Jonty and I would take a stump out to the field. He would practice hitting a single stump from every conceivable angle for hours on end. To achieve mastery, you need consistent, perfect repetitions. It takes almost 3000 perfect repetitions to transfer a skill from the conscious to the subconscious mind – to create the muscle memory I spoke of earlier. Since sport is played predominantly from your subconscious mind, it is vital that the mental programme governing your decision-making and execution be written through perfect practice.

In sport, we have a quote, **'Champions do the basics the best.'** The thing about basics is that they are boring to practice. James Clear sums it up well: *'The greatest threat to success is not failure but boredom.'*

Most people do not invest the time and energy necessary to master a skill because they are not sure if that investment will guarantee success. The truth is, even athletes do not have this guarantee. They wake up every day and push beyond their limits because it would be a great waste to get an opportunity you are not prepared for.

Don't Break the Chain

For the past ten years, I have been visiting the Kumbh Mela in India. It is the largest faith gathering in the world, attracting more than 100 million visitors over a period of forty-five days. Mystics, healers, yogis, some authentic and others questionable, all gather to celebrate the confluence of three rivers.

At the last gathering in Allahabad, India, I met a wonderful yogi. I was walking alongside the river when he caught my attention. There was nothing particularly different about him, except that the serenity on his face was admirable. I stood there for some time in awe of his tranquility. He may have felt me staring at him; eventually, he turned to me and invited me over.

His name was Kedharnath Saraswati Baba and he had been a renowned monk for more than forty years. I was intrigued. He was someone who had spent more than twelve hours' a day in meditation for over forty years. I could not even imagine the clarity of thought he would have. I asked him, '*Can you please teach me the art of meditation?*' This was the conversation that followed.

Kedharnath: What is your favourite food item?
Me: Chocolate (with a smile on my face).
Kedharnath: Have you ever tried to give it up?
Me: I have but I generally don't last more than two weeks. You see, I am an ultramarathon runner, and because of my excessive physical workload, I never quite felt the need to give up anything. I was already a vegan and I do not consume alcohol or drugs. This was my only real vice.
Kedharnath: Interesting. You want to learn to meditate. You want to master the art of controlling your mind.
Me: Yes.
Kedharnath: A piece of chocolate is laying on a table. Your eyes see it. Your hands reach out and pick it up. You eat it. **If you cannot control that which you see, how can you learn to control that which you cannot see.** Sometimes, you have to give something up to heal your body. Sometimes you have to give something up to strengthen your mind.

My mind was blown by the simplicity of his analogy and the wisdom it contained. He went on to explain that when you give something up or start a new habit, every single day that you refrain from it or stick to your routine is a reminder of how mentally strong you are. The longer the chain, the stronger your mind.

The incident reminded me of a powerful technique developed by one of the most successful comedians in the world, Jerry Seinfeld. According to *Forbes*, Seinfeld reached the peak of his earnings in 1998 when he grossed $267 millions in a year, a feat no other comedian has come close to achieving, even today. When asked how he managed to consistently churn out content that allowed him to stay ahead of the pack, he replied with a simple yet powerful strategy.

'The way to be a better comic is to create better jokes and the way to create better jokes is to write every day. I have a big wall calendar that has the whole year on one page and it hangs on a prominent wall. For every day that I write, I put a big red X over that day. After a few days you will have a chain and if you keep at it, the chain gets longer. You will like seeing that chain, especially after a few weeks. **Your only job is not to break the chain.'**

This became known as the Seinfeld Strategy. A simple, powerful technique to ensure you stick with the habits that lead to greatness. The Seinfeld Strategy is about consistency. Nothing else matters. Work schedules, travel schedules, prior commitments or even the quality of the work is irrelevant. The only thing that matters is that the chain cannot be broken.

Developing a strength is made up of the discipline, perseverance, and knowledge required to learn it. Mastering that strength is about the consistency of practice. There is no other formula.

Get into Your Zone

No chapter about defining strengths would be complete without some information about being 'in the zone' or achieving a state of 'flow.'

The father of flow science and author of the bestseller *Flow*, Mihaly Csikszentmihalyi, describes this state as *'being completely involved in an activity for its own sake. The ego falls away. Time flies. Every action, movement and thought follows inevitably from the previous one. Your whole being is involved and you're using your skills to the utmost.'*

In his book *Rise of the Superman*, Steven Kotler describes flow as a state when *'Every action, each decision, leads effortlessly, fluidly, seamlessly to the next. It's high-speed problem solving; it's being swept away by the river of ultimate performance.'*

In the world of sport, we refer to this state as being 'in the zone.' It is that all-encompassing state where your level of motivation to move from one task to another is at its peak, your decision-making process seems to operate independently of your conscious mind, and the results along every step of the way are in alignment with your goal. In a nutshell, there is an overwhelming sense of ease in how you operate.

As a performance coach, I had to search for the metrics that allowed me to engineer this optimal state of functioning for every athlete. While Kotler, Csikszentmihalyi, and other scientists have attempted to create a blueprint to achieve this state of flow, in reality there is no cookie cutter solution.

Eight Characteristics of Flow

1. Complete concentration on the task.
2. Clarity of goals and reward in mind and immediate feedback.

3. Transformation of time (speeding up/slowing down).
4. The experience is intrinsically rewarding.
5. Effortlessness and ease.
6. A balance between challenge and skills.
7. Actions and awareness are merged, losing self-conscious rumination.
8. A feeling of control over the task.

Csikszentmihalyi's eight characteristics sum up the essential preconditions for flow; however, there is an element that is often not spoken about. **A state of flow is rarely achieved the first time you practice a new skill.** In fact, a skill has to be deliberately and perfectly practised before that skill or strength becomes a part of our subconscious artillery.

As described previously, we develop a strength by applying knowledge (academic and experiential) to an existing talent, in combination with hours of deliberate practice, in order to translate it into a competitive advantage.

From my experience, achieving a flow state depends on the intensity, duration (time), and frequency (how often) of how you push yourself outside your comfort zone in practice. There is a direct relationship between the amount of time you spend outside your comfort zone and your ability to achieve a flow state. This explains why amateur athletes achieve flow rarely as compared to elite athletes. Professionals compete at a physiological level that is sub maximal, which means they demand more of themselves physiologically and psychologically in practice than in competition. While their state of arousal may be higher in competition, the physical and mental demands on their body are lower. This allows the mind to focus on the task at hand and achieve this feeling of being 'in the zone.'

In the eight characteristics of flow states, Csikszentmihalyi describes what can only be achieved through deliberate practice outside your comfort zone. Complete concentration on the task at hand is a by-product of intensity. The closer you get to tapping into the upper limits of your potential, the more clarity of thought you have. That feeling of being in control, the confluence between action and awareness, the sense of effortlessness and ease, understanding your immediate rewards, and the precision that accompanies that transformation over time are all consequences of consistently pushing your limits.

So what am I trying to say?

That feeling of getting 'in the zone' or achieving a 'flow state' is within an arm's reach for everyone. The key is to identify and understand a strength, then gather enough knowledge about how to improve it, and lastly, push its limits in practice. In the world of sport, we have a mantra: *'Everything you want in life is just outside your comfort zone.'*

There are millions of people who know their strengths and many of them are executing their strengths, but only a small percentage of these people ever achieve a state of flow.

Flow is reserved for those who are prepared to make the uncomfortable comfortable and the unfamiliar familiar, all in the pursuit of making the impossible possible.

Words cannot do justice to that feeling of bliss and that sense of achievement that accompanies this state. Authors, scientists, journalists, coaches, CEOs – they have all tried to describe this feeling. Many of them have probably never felt it as well. When you experience the clarity and stillness that accompanies flow, you will know in that moment; this cannot be described, but only felt.

I invite you to challenge yourself. Push yourself beyond every conceivable limits. Redefine yourself through practice. Find your flow. And experience a form of bliss so rare you will never settle for less.

If you want to discover your strengths and optimize your potential:

1. Take the StrengthFinder Assessment and answer the introspective questions
2. Email ten friends to find out your strengths
3. How 'coachable' are you?
4. Cultivate a monk-like discipline
5. Define your chain and commit to not breaking it
6. Push your limits
7. Find your flow

FOUR

Playing with Perspective
(Mind and Relationships)

We begin this chapter with what I call the Life Blueprint Exercise. (I will explain the name later.) This series of thirty-five questions is longer than some of the previous thought exercises, but don't let that scare you. It is meant to be completed quickly. It is a bit like a Rorschach Test in that it reveals underlying patterns in your thinking. And so, it is important to answer quickly and instinctively.

(The Rorschach Test is a psychological test in which subjects, perceptions of inkblots are recorded and then analyzed using psychological interpretation, complex algorithms or both. Psychologists use this test to examine an individual's personality characteristics and emotional functioning.)

A few other pointers on how to approach this exercise:

- Retreat to a safe place where you will be undisturbed for 15-30 minutes.
- Take a few moments to clear your mind and focus your attention.
- Be honest and transparent. Do not censor your thoughts.

- Avoid the temptation to overthink your answer. Begin writing within 5-10 seconds of reading the statement.
- Try to complete each statement in the order designed. Avoid revisiting the statements.
- Use the words that first come to your mind.

Are you ready? Here we go:

1. Life is ...

   ____

2. Women are ...

   ____

3. Men are ...

   ____

4. If only I could ...

   ____

5. I need to let go of ...

   ____

6. If I let go of #5, then ...

   ____

7. I am grateful for ...

   ____

8. I feel loved when ...

   ____

9. I feel powerful when ...

____

10. I feel content when ...

____

11. What I resist the most about myself is ...

____

12. What I resist the most about others is ...

____

13. If I complained less, then ...

____

14. If I accept myself more, then ...

____

15. I will come to terms with my past, if ...

____

16. My gift to others around me is ...

____

17. My self-worth comes from ...

____

18. I aspire to be more ...

____

19. If I had all the time in the world, I would ...

____

20. The best compliment I ever received was ...

____

21. I feel truly alive ______ % of the time

____

22. There are two types of people in the world:

    a) ____________________ and b) ____________________

23. I am a (one or two adjectives) ____________________ type of person.

24. I am afraid of ...

____

25. I lie the most about ...

____

26. I regret ...

____

27. Something I can never finish is ...

____

28. One rule I will never break is ...

____

29. I doubt ...

____

30. Love is ...

____

31. Revenge is ...

____

32. Privacy is...

____

33. Closure is ...

____

34. Pain is ...

____

35. Relationships are ...

____

The Life Blueprint is an exercise that draws our attention, in a nonjudgmental way, to the various lenses through which we view the world. Behind each of your responses to these questions are a set of assumptions – about yourself, about others, and about life. Again, this is not a matter of right or wrong. It is just important to understand your lenses. They filter your reality. In a sense, they create your reality.

Yet, most of the times, we are unaware of them. They are like a computer programme, operating silently and out of sight. They are so powerful precisely because they operate on a subconscious level.

The good news is that we are not stuck with our current lenses. We can reprogramme ourselves. In recent years, scientists have discovered that our brains have a remarkable ability to adapt and change. Due to this property of *neuroplasticity*[1], we can quite literally rewire our brains. But in order to change these lenses, and the programmes behind them, we must be aware of them. We must bring the subconscious to our conscious awareness. That is the purpose of this exercise.

I call it the Life Blueprint exercise because, just like the DNA encoded in our cells is a kind of blueprint for how our body is to grow and develop, so these deeply encoded programmes form a kind of hidden blueprint for our lives.

If this sounds like an overstatement, think about it: the lens through which you view your world is significant. It determines your current reality. This exercise isn't designed to question or judge your reality, or how you view the world – but to understand it.

I created it out of necessity, when I felt I had hit rock bottom. I was curious as to why certain patterns kept repeating themselves, resulting in a string of poor relationships. Spirituality taught me to accept reality and learn from every situation. I was doing exactly that but was still acutely aware that **I cannot fix that which I am not prepared to change**. Moreover, **I cannot change what I am not consciously aware of**.

After using the Life Blueprint exercise, I was able to put a magnifying glass on the perspectives that framed my reality. My insights hit me like a ton of bricks. Certain lenses or perspectives at play were creating my reality. Lenses, I did not consciously choose. Lenses, I did not even know existed. My reality was manifesting in accordance with the subconscious programmes that were created by those around me, by my pain, and by my childhood. For the first time, using the Life Blueprint exercise, I had the power to choose how I would view the world. This is what the exercise does. It puts you in a position to ascertain if a certain perspective is going to serve the best version of yourself. It gives you back the power you never knew you had.

Deciphering Your Lenses

The thirty-five statements in the Life Blueprint exercise reflect how you think, feel, and react in every situation. Your answers unmask the lenses through which you view the world. Each answer reveals a code written into your subconscious by an experience. These experiences could be recent, or they could go back to your childhood.

These realizations can be potent. As a patient who did the exercise said, *'This is the first time I had to ever think about what made me feel powerful, loved, content or worthy.'*

The Blueprint forces you to put a magnifying glass on the small things that control your life, perhaps those things that determine your self-worth, or perhaps elements of your personality you are afraid to reveal. I have had patients break down crying when they realized how insecure they were, or how a particular childhood incident had moulded the way they see the world now.

Each answer could have multiple layers. I would encourage you to scratch below the surface of every answer. Can you remember a particular incident that created that lens?

No matter how innocuous the answer may seem, it could potentially be a clue to other destructive patterns.

Let me illustrate the process of deciphering these answers with an example:
A female patient completed the statement, *Women are ...* as follows: *Women are giving.*

On the surface, the answer appears simple. However, if we view this answer as a lens, it reveals an entire way of looking at the world, and her role in life. Digging deeper into this answer sent us down the rabbit hole. Her response indicates that giving is at the very core of her identity. I began to explore this lens with a few follow-up questions:

- How comfortable are you with receiving attention or love?
- Are you able to speak up when something is bothering you?
- Do you feel like you are responsible for maintaining the harmony in every relationship?
- Are you afraid that if you speak up and upset those close to you, they may leave?

By exploring the underlying narrative behind this lens, we were able to identify a pattern of emotional deprivation deeply rooted in her childhood and upbringing. Her self-worth had been eroded by her parents who were emotionally unavailable. As a result, she grew up afraid of losing loved ones, which manifested a fear of being authentic and speaking in her mind. She doubted her self-worth, and to prevent the world from seeing this, she placed the needs of everyone else above her own. Giving is a beautiful thing, but not if it comes at the expense of eroding your spirit. Her love and caring for others was not in balance with a healthy love of self.

It is difficult to predict which statement might provide a window into a destructive subconscious pattern. For this reason, I encourage you to explore each lens in depth. Hopefully, the example I just gave will help you in your investigation of your own responses. Remember, the exercise is not meant only to identify destructive patterns. It is designed to put a magnifying glass on the lenses. You may conclude that some of the lenses are healthy and work well for you. After exploring a lens, you are welcome to keep that lens in play if you believe it is serving the Higher You.

You can use these additional questions as a roadmap in examining each lens:

- How does this lens make me feel? (Happy, neutral or sad)
- What was the incident that brought this lens into play?
- Now that I am aware of this lens, how does it make me feel?
- If I had the option to change it, what would I replace it with?
- Is this lens in alignment with my core values (as discussed in 'Self-love')?
- Will this lens help me become a better version of myself?
- What is the feeling this lens invokes in others?

The Actor and the Audience

I love exploring and playing with lenses. It is helpful to realize that behind each lens and each programme is a narrative – a narrative rooted in the past, and one that reflects a certain view of the world. Remember, the brain likes stories. We think in stories, and the stories we tell ourselves (often subconsciously) shape our view of the world, our thoughts and emotions, and our actions.

Now that we have introduced the idea of uncovering the hidden narratives in your responses to the Life Blueprint exercise, you can go deeper and start choosing the lens through which you would like to view those narratives. In most cases, we do not make conscious, deliberate choices about the lenses we use to view the world. Sometimes those lenses are chosen for us as part of our upbringing. Or we simply absorb them as part of our environment, like the air we breathe. It all happens below the level of our conscious awareness – which is why bringing these stories to the surface is such a powerful exercise.

Now that you have begun to identify your lenses, and the narratives and programmes behind them, you can choose to see through different lenses. If you have ever visited an optician for an eye exam, you would have experienced a flipper lens, which allows the optician to toggle between various lenses and find the perfect match for your vision. Similarly, once we become aware of our psychological lenses, we can mindfully choose to toggle from one lens to the other.

One thing I have found particularly helpful in my own life, and in my work with others, is to imagine toggling from the lens of the actor in our lives to the lens of an audience. Normally, we see ourselves as the lead actor of our life's drama: deeply immersed in the thoughts and emotions of the moment. Sometimes this is healthy. But at other times, our emotions swallow us up and we lose perspective. We need to step back and take stock. We need to imagine ourselves as a member of the audience, watching from the shadows of the theatre. From that distance, we can view ourselves objectively and dispassionately, without judgment of ourselves, or others.

When you think about it, this is really just another way of looking at how mindfulness works. **When you master the art of mindfulness, something beautiful happens. You develop the ability to cultivate an awareness that is non-reactive.** You become a witness to the events of your life, through a nonjudgmental lens. The witness can split the narrative from the emotion and observe each element independently. This does not mean that your troubles will disappear, but there is a high probability that they will not trouble you as much anymore. This is the power of mindfulness. It allows you to hold an object in your attention long enough to view it from multiple perspectives.

When you cultivate the ability to move between the actor and the audience, lenses become your playground. They can challenge you to move outside your comfort zone or give you a deeper sense of comfort at a difficult time in your life. We all use lenses to inspire us, motivate us, comfort us, and challenge us. Unfortunately, most times, we are unaware of how they are operating.

Just remember, we cannot achieve mindful awareness of our emotions and our lenses overnight. The practice of mindfulness must begin with the basics: with meditation and breath work. These practices help us train our attention. By focusing on the breath, we are able to strengthen our ability to hold our attention undistractedly. The mind may wander at times. Each time, the meditator draws attention back to the breath. With time, this process becomes easier. The mind becomes tranquil and eventually the ability to focus attention requires less effort.

You can then expand your awareness, becoming aware of the flow of air in and out of your lungs, and the associated physiological changes. The temperature difference between the air entering your body and the air leaving your body. The gentle rise and fall of your belly or chest. Your heartbeat. The more your practice, the more you notice. The deeper your attention, the deeper the insight. Insight is the second powerful tool that accompanies mindfulness. As your attention expands, you also become mindful of your emotional states, and the physical sensations associated with them. From there, you learn to witness your present emotions, and those connected with the past, from a place of calmness and clarity.

The more you practice the fundamentals of mindfulness, the more you will be able to shift your lens effortlessly from that of actor to that of audience.

Focus versus Perspective

The purpose of this chapter is to reveal the lens through which you view the world.

As you continue to work with the Life Blueprint exercise and explore your personal lenses, it is helpful to understand the difference between focus and perspective.

Focus: is that which is the centre of our attention. *What are we looking at?*

Perspective: the position from which we draw our attention to the point of focus. *From what vantage point are we looking at it?*

Because mindfulness allows us to become a witness to the events in our mind, it gives us the power to experience these events independent of judgment or interpretation. As your awareness deepens, so will your ability to experience the interplay between the actor and the audience. With time, you will realize that you have the power to choose one of the multiple perspectives within the audience as well. You can also choose the perspective of one of the other 'actors' on stage. When you cultivate this skill, your perception of any event in your life will change drastically.

Perception: the interpretation of a situation from a specific point of view.

After years of meditation, I began to see the world through many lenses. I can now choose the experiences I would like to be fully immersed in (actor) and those I would like to keep at an emotional arm's length (audience). Not only does this help me understand and process the events in my life, it plays a vital role in my work as a therapist and sports scientist.

In professional sports, we always strategize from the view point of our opponent. What would they be expecting us to do? How can we counteract their strengths? Where and how do we bring in the element of surprise? Knowing your strengths is important but strategizing through the lens of your opponent allows you to understand how you can best leverage those strengths. It is a delicate balance that can only be achieved through perspective.

Healing is tough and sacred. I have encountered many patients who have a desire to heal but are just not willing to heal. Desire does not always equate to willingness. These are all lenses for me. Sometimes, I guide them to heal from pain; at other times, I teach them to function with it. There is no cookie cutter approach to healing. However, **a mindfulness practice allows you to view the world through a wide-angle lens that captures every detail.** It gives you options you previously were unaware of.

Here are a few more exercises to help you train perspective

Think of a situation you are currently going through. It could be something at work, or a family problem.

- Now list down everyone impacted by this situation.
- Spend a few minutes looking at the situation through their lenses.
- What are their emotions, associated with the situation?
- How does each person's reality stack up against yours?
- Could I possibly view the situation from their point of view?
- Would it help me or make my current reality seem worse?

The more you play with lenses, the larger your perspective. The greater your options, the higher the probability of success.

Think of two things you will most likely regret twenty years from today.

I love this question because it immediately changes your lens from your current reality to twenty years later. If you are anything like the 100,000+ people I have asked this question to, you would have one if not both of these answers on your list.

- Not taking care of your health.
- Not spending enough time with loved ones.

In this case, switching the lens puts you in a position of strength. Armed with the knowledge from this lens, you can now make the requisite changes to ensure this potentially disastrous reality does not manifest. A simple lens switch puts you in a position to change something that you may have regretted down the line.

Victim versus Player Mentality

The *victim mentality* is one of the most debilitating states of mind. It is a dysfunctional mindset in which the individual seeks persecution in order to gain attention or sympathy or avoid taking responsibility of their own actions or circumstances. People who struggle with victim mentality are convinced that their life is beyond their control. They perceive life as happening *to* them.[2]

Using a sporting reference, you cannot influence the outcome of a game from the side lines. When you are on the field or in the game, you can take measures to change the outcome. This is the *player mentality*. An individual who sees their role as active and pivotal in the outcome of their life. They determine their own destiny. Player mentality is an all-empowering state. Victim mentality renders the individual powerless. Players mentality is about accountability and responsibility. Victim mentality is about blame. You feel the entire world is against you and you can do nothing about it[3].

Both of these mental states are lenses. One individual chooses to see the world from a position of opportunity and the other from a position of threat. We have all played the victim card many times in our lives. The victim card preserves our innocence, at least in our minds, which is why we choose it. Who doesn't like to feel innocent when their world is falling apart? But through mindfulness and awareness, we are able to shift this lens. If you are someone who sees the silver lining in every situation, you are testament to the fact that changing a lens is not only possible, but empowering as well. **You are a representation of the hope the world needs to see.**

The victim and the player, the actor and the audience, the old and the young. These and many more lenses are at your disposal. In the next chapter, we are going to explore more deeply how certain lenses can become so ingrained in our psyche that they turn into life-long psychological programmes – shaping our worldview, our expectations for life, and how we approach our relationships. Often rooted in our early childhood, these programmes, if left unnoticed, can sabotage every relationship in our lives.

We are going to use our lenses to heal these patterns.

The Infinity Loop

At this point, we can take the Life Blueprint exercise to a deeper level. We can begin choosing which lenses are helpful and healthy and work for us; and we can discard unhealthy lenses and replace them with new ones.

To review: The lenses that you are learning to identify are enmeshed in a particular narrative, a story about how life works, a way of seeing the world. As we internalize that story at a subconscious level, it starts to operate like a programme. The subconscious mind that runs most of our mental programmes is automatic and does not distinguish between good and bad, or right and wrong. It simply runs a programme that has been installed. If for any reason a particular programme isn't serving you well, you have to first identify it and bring it back into the conscious mind. You can then in essence reinstall a new programme through the deliberate practice of new habits. **I call this the Infinity Loop: The secret to healing and performance**. Once those habits become second nature, you will be operating from a new programme – but a healthy one, and one of your own choosing.

I have used this Infinity Loop with some of the best athletes in the world. They compete from the fast, subconscious mind; and practice from the slow, mindful conscious mind. They use habits and routines (implemented by the conscious mind) to shape or reprogramme their unconscious mind. They also make use of the technique of visualization.

We can install new programmes by way of new habits, and also by way of visualization. When we vividly conjure a positive video loop in our minds and play it over and over again, the brain responds just as it would to a real-life experience. We are rewriting the brain and creating new mental habits. Visualization is a kind of mental workout that treats the brain like a muscle.

The conscious mind allows you to make changes in your habits – both habits of routine, and habits of mind – that shape your subconscious programming. In other words, the conscious mind literally designs the programmes that drive the subconscious mind. In sport, as is in life, the Infinity Loop is the secret to becoming a better version of yourself.

A mindfulness practice can help you cultivate a more refined type of awareness, one that distinguishes between reality as it is, and an emotional, distorted version of reality. Through the clarity and focus that accompanies your mindfulness practice, you will be able to choose between being an actor and an audience to your own personal narrative. The Infinity Loop puts you in a position of strength. You can choose the emotions you wish to immerse in, and those you wish to simply be a witness to. Mindfulness allows you to shift your perspectives. Change your lenses. You can now act instead of reacting to every emotion and situation you find yourself in.

This is particularly helpful in the realm of relationships. In many cases, the unhealthy lenses we need to change are inseparable from our relationship. In 'Circles of Connection' we covered Lester Luborsky's Core Conflict Theory, which demonstrates that an individual simply wants to be understood, empathized with, respected, valued, and treated fairly. **Every relationship can survive arguments**

and fights – but it cannot survive the loss of safety and security.

If a relationship has deteriorated to the point where one or both individuals feel devalued, lost, disrespected, or misunderstood, it is likely that the relationship is being dictated by the functions of the subconscious mind. This means that every single aspect, from living together and spending time with the family to dinner table conversations, all operate from a place of mundane (and unmindful) routine. Both parties go through the motions, the relationship is on autopilot. The illusion that things are alright may persist for some time – until one person wakes up and realizes all is not well, or until a long-simmering tension rises to the surface. One or both will experience a loss of safety and security. They will sense that the other is there in name and body only but is not present emotionally.

You have to be emotionally present to ensure an individual is understood, respected, valued, and treated fairly. To be emotionally present is a consequence of conscious, mindful awareness.

Therefore, if you want a relationship to evolve, you must create a loop between the activities of the conscious and subconscious minds.

In simple terms, this means mindfully changing the routine of those little things that you take for granted in the relationship. **When you start to become mindful of the little things, you bring a programme from the fast, automatic subconscious mind to the slow, mindful, conscious mind.** Through the awareness of the conscious mind, you can rewrite these programmes before they get reinstalled in the subconscious mind. This is the Infinity Loop as it applies to our relationships.

It is impossible to overstate the power of learning to change your lenses. In his classic book *Man's Search for Meaning,* Viktor Frankl helps his fellow prisoners shift their perspectives. The men in those concentration camps believed that the real opportunities in their lives had passed. In reality, there was an opportunity and a challenge. Viktor helped them reposition the experiences, find hope in those opportunities and achieve a state of inner triumph. The shift in perspective brought with it a sense of hope and meaning. In the words of Nietzsche, *'He who has a why to live for can bear almost any how.'*

Frankl and Nietzsche are both teaching us an important lesson. **When you cultivate the ability to shift your perspective, you elevate yourself to a place of hope, a place where you can endure almost anything.**

If you want to learn to use different lenses:

1. Cultivate a mindful practice using either breath work or meditation.
2. Practice using the actor and audience lenses for situations in your life.
3. Complete the Life Blueprint exercise.
4. Use the explorative questions to decipher each lens.
5. Play with the other lenses in the suggestive exercises.

FIVE

Freeing Yourself from Destructive Patterns (Mind, Relationships, Environment)

Write down three things you wish you were told as a child:

1.

2.

3.

In the previous chapter, we explored the importance of learning to mindfully switch our lenses. Through practices like meditation and breath work, we learned how to calm the mind, push away toxic thoughts, and stay grounded in the present. That process brings with it insights that allow us to see things as they are and not as we want them to be.

This chapter builds on that discussion of lenses. As we have seen, a lens is not just a way of looking at the world and our life; it usually has a story or narrative attached to it. That story often has its roots in early childhood experiences; some of them traumatic. We told ourselves a certain story because it helped us make sense of the world and helped us cope with a difficult experience. This is one of the reasons the brain likes stories.

The problem begins when those old stories and lenses get stuck and fail to evolve as we grow older. We begin to superimpose an old, outdated story on new experiences. What was once an effective coping mechanism at a previous point in our lives no longer serves us well in the present. Quite to the contrary, that old mental model prevents us from seeing anything that doesn't conform to our established ideas of the world. Instead, it only looks for facts that confirm pre-existing beliefs. It is a view of the world and of life that has become frozen in time. It is no longer a healthy coping mechanism, but what psychologists call a *maladaptive pattern,* one that blocks you from becoming the best version of yourself.

That, in a nutshell, is the science of **schemas**, a term in psychology that encapsulates everything we have been talking about. *A schema is a lens, a narrative, a mental model, and a coping mechanism.* As pioneered by psychologist Jeffrey Young, the study of schema has become a school of therapy in its own right – one geared towards helping people break out of life-long, self-defeating emotional and behavioural patterns. Technically, schemas are not behavioural traits themselves. Rather, our behavioural patterns are a response to our schema or lenses. Change the schema – in other words, write a new story for yourself and your behaviour will adapt in time.

Before we move on, let's look back and integrate this new terminology into our previous discussions of balance.

One way of looking at schema is that they emerge as a way to help us create balance and equilibrium, a foothold of sanity, in an otherwise chaotic and imbalanced reality. That is all well and good. But if the associated coping mechanism becomes frozen and fails to evolve as we and our life circumstances do, we have a mismatch, like a square peg in a round hole. We try to impose a fixed, unchanging coping strategy on a fluid, changing reality. We are, in the terms we used earlier, trying to create a static balance in a fluid, dynamic situation.

Or, to use another metaphor, it is like trying to build a new house on an old foundation. Your old lenses may have outworn their usefulness. It just might be time to replace them with new lenses that reflect who you are today, and the reality of the life you aspire for.

By way of illustration, let's briefly examine the lifecycle of a very common schema, of someone who has grown up with a parent suffering from alcoholism or another form of substance abuse. Such a household will typically be chaotic and unpredictable – loving and stable one minute, volatile and perhaps even violent the next. So the young person growing up in that environment accommodates to the chaos; in a sense, they make friends with it. Later in life, they subconsciously or unknowingly seek out chaos, and violence, unpredictable relationships. Deep inside, the person, now an adult, knows these relationships aren't healthy. But they are familiar. In a strange way, they have become a kind of comfort zone. Such a person needs to learn to write a new story – to replace the schema that says chaos is inevitable with one that says stability is possible.

As we move ahead now, we will look deeper within, into some of the maladaptive patterns that block you from becoming the best version of yourself. These subconscious patterns can sabotage your productivity at work, your intimacy in relationships, and your overall self-worth. These patterns might include the following: a fear of failure, a fear of rejection, inexplicable mistrust, self-doubt and self-criticism, the inability to express empathy. These are just a few of the mental models your subconscious may have created to interpret the chaos around it.

More than a decade ago when I decided to explore inner child work and subconscious programmes, it was not the obvious route for a sports scientist. While the rest of my colleagues were focused on flow states, peak performance, and mental imagery, I was turning to inner child work. Partly because I recognized the need to heal myself, but also because I was intrigued by how my athletes were themselves often the greatest obstacle to fully realizing their own potential. For example, a tennis player completely self-destructs after an unforced error in a big game. Such an error is reasonable cause for being upset; but when you lose control of your ability to refocus on the next point, it is a problem. When you are aware of this pattern but unable to stop it, it becomes even more paralyzing. I wanted to explore the subconscious destructive patterns driving this behaviour. Much of my learnings have strong and relevant applications beyond the word of sports and business. They can also help you heal your life and achieve a state of bliss, contentment, and happiness.

Through mindful awareness of schemas, you can empower yourself. As Jon Kabat-Zinn says, *'There is far more right with us than wrong with us.'* **Through cultivated awareness, you can reconnect with your purest, most authentic, higher self.** This is what you can look forward to.

> *The work of Jeffery Young and his colleagues in Schema Therapy provided me with a blueprint that helped me identify patterns that were sabotaging any chance of a healthy, happy life. Schema Therapy helped me heal from pain that was more than twenty years old. This is why I want to share with you, a brief outline of the science. This chapter was conceptualized to highlight a unique component of cognitive psychology. If you feel drawn towards Schema Therapy, I recommend working with a qualified therapists in the field. I have a full list of reading material and additional resources at the end of the book.*

In this chapter, we will discover:

- Understanding Schema
- Coping Mechanisms
- Ten Common Maladaptive Emotional Schemas
- Self-help Techniques to Reprogramme New Habits

During a Healing Circle in Goa, an attendee, Louise, asked me: 'How can I learn to be a better partner? I have been betrayed four times in relationships despite being a loving, loyal, compassionate, and caring partner.'

'You are asking the wrong question,' I told her. 'The right question is why do I always choose people who betray me?'

Again, the brain likes familiarity. As a case in point, the **Ellsberg Paradox** shows that individuals prefer a known probability of winning (even when that probability is low) over an ambiguous probability (even when that probability is high).

In a nutshell, **the devil we know is better than the devil we don't know.**

Herein lies the paradox of the mind. Your conscious mind yearns for one thing, but your subconscious mind prompts you to think and act in a manner that prevents that reality from manifesting. Louise yearns for the love, safety, and security of a healthy relationship. Her conscious mind is aware of this and is searching for it. Her subconscious mind, on the other hand, is drawn to a personality type that, while not conducive to a healthy relationship, is at least familiar to her. So her pattern of unhealthy relationships repeats itself.

This brings me to the seventh realization.

Realization #7

To change your current reality, you have to make the unfamiliar familiar.

Understanding Schemas

A schema is a deep unconditional belief about oneself, one's relationship to others and one's relationship to their environment. It is a mental model or subconscious programme that develops during early childhood or adolescence but persists throughout an individual's adult life. Schemas help us create order among the chaos by creating a framework through which we perceive and then act. They are literally shortcuts in our brain that operate from the subconscious mind, which means that we don't have to pay attention to them for them to operate efficiently.

Emotional Maladaptive Schemas (EMS) are self-sabotaging, pervasive patterns that are triggered from one's early childhood. In some way, together they form *an infinite loop, constantly reminding you of a need in your life, but at the same time sabotaging every attempt to satisfy that need.* Most of us have at least one if not a cluster of schemas at play, but likely are not aware of them. Nonetheless, they can play a negative and even destructive role in our lives.

And so, they can be elusive and lay hidden in our daily lives. The fear of failure that prevents you from starting a new venture, the inner voice that makes you question your self-worth and constantly searches for reassurance, the feeling of entitlement and the lack of empathy that accompanies it, the fear of loneliness, the fear that you will never be understood or heard. These are all subconscious schemas that surface from time to time.

If we are to free ourselves from these schemas, we must

first identify them. In therapy, I have found that putting a magnifying glass on the early life experiences that bring these schemas to the surface.

There are four life experiences that may give rise to an emotional schema.

1. **Toxic Frustration of Needs:** The lack of stability, understanding, and love gives rise to deprivation and abandonment schemas.
2. **Traumatization:** When children are harmed, controlled, victimized, and criticized, it results in mistrust, defectiveness, and subjugation schemas.
3. **Too Much of a Good Thing:** When children are given too much of something that would be healthy in moderation, they develop an entitlement schema.
4. **Selective Internalization:** When children selectively identify and internalize a parent's thoughts, feelings, experiences, and schemas, it often results in a vulnerability schema.

Every child has certain basic core emotional needs that must be satisfied. When these needs are met, a child can thrive. The absence of these needs is what gives rise to an emotional schema. According to Jeffery Young, there are **Five Types of Core Emotional Needs** that every child needs:

1. Safety, stability, nurturance, and acceptance
2. Autonomy, competence, and a sense of identity
3. Freedom to express valid needs and emotions
4. Spontaneity and play
5. Realistic limits and self-control

Every schema has a unique signature. For each person the trigger is different. The feelings and emotions that accompany them are particular to that individual. The common element is the way you take control of your life, recreating the emotions of the traumatizing incident that gave birth to the schema in the first place.

It is important to understand that schemas were created to protect you. They were your mind's innate survival and adaptive mechanisms. A child who feels that it was only his/her achievements that earned the affection of his/her parents learns to push himself/herself harder in an effort to be successful, because success equates to love. Your mind created these schemas to prevent you from feeling the pain of that void. The obvious question is: **if they are a solution to a problem, why should they need healing?**

Emotional schemas are only half-solutions. They are a band-aid that momentarily eases the pain, but that rarely addresses the core predicament. The child who equates success with love will constantly push himself/herself, emotionally, physically, and mentally to achieve success. That is the band-aid. The core problem is that the child/adult must learn to disassociate his/her self-worth from the outcome of the project. He/she is complete and worthy of love, irrespective of the outcome. Healing this at the core allows the individual to find balance in their life, to make peace with being less compulsively driven. A schema amplifies a single emotional need, while rendering you oblivious to other core emotional needs. It leads to an imbalanced emotional life. The goal of schema healing is to decrease the intensity and influence of these patterns in an individual's life – to replace maladaptive coping styles with more adaptable behaviour patterns.

Coping Mechanisms

A coping mechanism is exactly that. A technique which was once a healthy survival mechanism for a child has now evolved into a maladaptive coping strategy with time – like a crutch that is useful at first, but then cripples and weakens us. Every individual's coping strategy varies from schema to schema. Exactly why an individual chooses a particular coping style isn't exactly clear. Sometimes temperament plays a big role. Psychology has recognized that passive individuals surrender to their schemas while those with an aggressive temperament tend to overcompensate.

There are three main maladaptive coping mechanisms: **surrender, avoidance,** and **overcompensation.**

When an individual *surrenders* to their schema, that schema is accepted as the truth. As a result, the emotional consequences of that schema are relived throughout adulthood. These individuals welcome people into their lives who are likely to treat them as their parents did. They then relate those individuals to their parents which exacerbates the situation. It's no wonder the relationship is destined for failure.

Probably, one of the most recognizable coping mechanisms is *avoidance*. These individuals avoid situations that could trigger their schemas at all costs. As a result, they struggle with intimate relationships, have challenges at work, and immense difficulty being vulnerable. They are highly prone to withdrawal symptoms, excessive autonomy, addictive self-soothing, and substance abuse.

The third coping mechanism is *overcompensation*, in which individuals resist the schema by vigorously counterattacking it. In an attempt to not feel overwhelmed, helpless or vulnerable, this coping strategy makes them insensitive to the feelings of others. Aggression, excessive self-assertion, status seeking, hostility, and dominance are strongly associated with overcompensation.

Schemas determine the way we think, feel, and act. Irrespective of whether we are aware of them or not, they influence how we process every experience in our lives. The phenomenon of **Schema Chemistry** describes how we are unfortunately drawn towards people who trigger our schemas. It comes back to the subconscious mind's affinity for familiarity. Despite the fact that those individuals make us feel somewhat misunderstood, deprived, unloved, unworthy, and disrespected, we are drawn to the suffering. But there is a silver lining.

Light at the End of the Tunnel

Maladaptive emotional schemas and coping mechanisms were learnt. If something was learnt, it can be unlearnt and relearnt. The only prerequisite for healing these schemas is willingness. You must come with an uncompromising willingness to be honest, to scratch below the surface of your emotional pain, to be vulnerable, to let go, to trust.

We all have had days when we just didn't feel like exercising. We were exhausted or had a long day, and the idea of pushing ourselves physically was not appealing. Sometimes we convince ourselves to do just fifteen minutes of exercise, and once we have started we feel okay enough to finish an entire session. This happens because the greatest resistance is in the beginning. After we start, the initial success and the momentum it creates makes the whole journey that much easier.

Emotional healing and letting go is no different. Once you bring your awareness to those self-destructive patterns, the need to heal them surfaces. From here, feelings of inner peace, of confidence in your healing, and of liberation from the old pain override the initial inertia of the struggle. Like a caterpillar evolving into a butterfly, you too will fall in love with your new evolution.

A Note to Self

Healing is tough, and it requires a special type of courage. To pull back the veil on deep emotional pain is never easy. The fact that you got this far is truly inspirational.

You are stronger than you think and kinder than you realize.

The courage to walk down this path is testament to everything your soul desires.

The love, the compassion, the gentleness and the empathy. **This is you**.

Be gentle with your soul as you embark on a journey of self-discovery. Try to be emotionally present and aware.

Avoid the tendency to judge. Feel every raw emotion. Explore the depths of every thought, feeling and emotion. Look for patterns.

- Does each emotion bring back a memory or a particular feeling?
- How do you feel when you revisit these emotions and memories?
- Do you recognize similar feelings in your day-to-day life?

Every schema has a unique signature for each of us. Even the manner in which we cope with them is nuanced. I will describe ten common schemas in terms of how they manifest. You may find it easier to recognize a schema through its behaviour signatures.

As we move through the schema descriptions, try to employ the lens of an audience first.

Watch for similarities, recognize patterns, identify your personal coping mechanisms, and try to interpret how they play out in your life. The lens of a witness is always a great place from which to view pain and heal.

Common Maladaptive Emotional Schemas

1. Emotional Deprivation:

A child growing up in an environment in which one or both parents are emotionally unavailable (due to work or social commitments, or preoccupation with their own interests, perhaps substance abuse, or simply being over burdened by their problems) might well develop a core belief of deprivation. **Deprivation is when a child feels that no**

matter how much they speak or ask for something, no one hears them. Such a child feels their needs will never be met.

There are three forms of deprivation:

Deprivation of Nurturance: Absence of attention, affection, warmth or companionship

Deprivation of Empathy: Absence of understanding, listening, self-disclosure and a mutual sharing of feelings with others

Deprivation of Protection: Absence of strength, direction and guidance from others

Deprivation in adults can sabotage any healthy relationship. Those who suffer from it are hypersensitive to signs of not being noticed, respected, or valued. This can trigger anger but that can quickly transition to feelings of loneliness and sadness.

A patient, John, used the Life Blueprint exercise to diagnose his deprivation schema. He completed the sentence, 'Relationships are' with the word 'giving'. When we analyzed his early childhood, we understood that the deprivation was created by his father who was constantly travelling. The relationship with his mother was toxic and eroded his self-worth. Giving, in every relationship, became a coping mechanism to shield his pain, loneliness and sadness.

Deprivation can also present itself in the form of resentment. When the patient feels their needs are not met, they can become angry and demanding, making it difficult for people to empathize with them. Once again, we see the paradox in which someone's behaviour undermines their core need.

Deprivation is like a black hole. No matter how much people try to satisfy your needs, the individual will always feel discontent. A loop of self-loathing prevents them from clearly articulating their needs. In fact, they might feel that others should intuitively know and understand their needs without them having to communicate it.

Julia, a patient whose younger brother was terminally ill, developed a version of deprivation in which the need to care served as a way to cope with the inadequate parenting of her past. Julia felt she had to parent herself, and those around her as well. This coping mechanism can kill the sexual intimacy in a relationship between partners. This need to give does not remove the core deprivation of not having one's emotional needs met. Giving once again becomes a façade behind which they hide.

The subtleties in deprivation schema can vary from person to person. To assess if this schema is applicable to you, try to recognize if you are feeling neglected in some way. To see this, you must let go of your ego. Beyond the success, the giving to others, the emotional strong façade you put up, what is the core feeling you identify with?

When you identify the schema and your coping strategy, you are well on your way to healing yourself. *Mindfully drawing your attention to the way you think, feel, and act in response to the core feeling of neglect will slowly help you start your healing journey.*

2. Abandonment or Instability

Christopher recalls having the most remarkable relationship with his father, until his parents divorced and his dad had to move out. His mother was so preoccupied with pulling her life together that young Christopher could not help but feel abandoned and alone. From that moment on, he has battled loneliness and the fear of being rejected.

The abandonment schema is expressed as a fear of being alone, and is accompanied by deep feelings of sadness, loneliness, worry, panic, and resentment. It often manifests from an early childhood experience. One or both parents could have been emotionally unavailable; a parent dies; perhaps divorce forces a parent to leave; or a distracted, unreliable parent is never there for the child. All of these can trigger deep abandonment issues.

A signature coping mechanism in such cases is clinginess. There is a need for constant reassurance that their partner loves them and is not going to leave. This fear manifesting as clinginess actually ends up driving loved ones away. The pattern may become cyclic and, after a few bad relationships, the person will feel like they cannot trust being loved and grow emotionally unavailable. They will build walls that keep them at arm's length and this in itself can trigger intimacy issues.

Sarah's home environment was extremely toxic. Every time her mother voiced her opinion, her father got angry, lashed out, and left for days or weeks on end. Sarah developed an abandonment schema with an innate fear of speaking about her emotional needs. Her fear of loneliness prevented her from voicing her opinion, which she worried might push a partner away. Abandonment schema will prevent you from trusting your feelings and intuition. You will allow yourself to be disrespected, devalued, and misunderstood, all in an effort to avoid being left alone or abandoned.

The abandonment schema may apply to you if you fear being left alone or abandoned. If you are hypersensitive every time a loved one travels, hesitate to speak your mind for fear your partner may leave, need constant reassurance from a loved one, or sabotage your relationships with excessive clinginess, you may need to heal an abandonment schema. *You can learn to become comfortable with yourself; more importantly, you can learn to trust the quality of the relationships you have built.*

3. Defectiveness/Unlovability/Shame

The defectiveness schema is also known as the 'unlovability' schema. **At the core of this schema is a feeling of being flawed and not worthy of love. There is a general sense of 'I am not enough.'** Individuals with a defectiveness schema are in constant fear of being exposed. They tell themselves, 'If people really get to know me, they won't like me.'

Mary grew up in a small village in India. She is small in stature, which became an obsession with her parents. Convinced that she had a growth defect, her parents took her from doctor to doctor in search of a solution. It wasn't long before Mary became the centre of every discussion, and not in a heartwarming manner. She recalls this with shame and humiliation. Her parents convinced her that there was something wrong with her.

Fast forwarding twenty-five years, Mary has no more than three people who are close to her. 'I don't like people and I don't enjoy letting people close to me. Life is pointless, so why bother in cultivating healthy relationships.' The defectiveness schema sabotages her ability to connect with people because she fears that if people get to know who she is, they will not love her.

The defectiveness schema is born from hyper-critical, insulting, or demeaning parents. Sometimes, in an effort to push you to become successful, they instill a deep sense of unworthiness in you. The core emotions associated with defectiveness are shame, and sometimes humiliation. When you feel that your weaknesses are being exposed, an overwhelming feeling of shame forces you to retract.

Someone with defectiveness schema struggles to be open about their thoughts and feelings. They lack self-confidence, and an inner voice constantly questions their self-worth. The feeling of not being deserving or unworthy will consume any chance of happiness.

People with defectiveness expect the worst. In relationships, instead of being present and enjoying every experience, their mind fixates on possible rejection. It is one of the foremost causes of intimacy problems in a relationship. They simply do not trust the process of being vulnerable and sincerely believe that being authentic will precipitate their downfall.

If you suffer from defectiveness, mindful awareness of the

patterns that trigger this schema is important. Often, the signs are subtle, mostly in the form of negative self-talk. You have to believe that you are worthy of love. As an exercise, I encourage my patients to start becoming comfortable with receiving love. Allow those around you to spoil you and let you know the positive impact you have made in their lives. With a few close friends, start to expose your vulnerabilities and be mindful of how they react. *Healing this schema is about becoming open to feeling and expressing, but also knowing that one's opinion of you is simply that – just an opinion and not the gospel truth. You can heal this schema and unlock the best version of yourself.*

4. Subjugation

This pattern is often born from extremely dominating parenting. **A child has no voice with respect to what they like or what they would like to do.** Every decision is taken by the parents and this pattern goes beyond what is considered normal. The child loses every sense of autonomy.

I suffered from a subjugation schema – not through my upbringing but from having grown up in an apartheid South Africa. The core belief in this schema is that 'my voice does not matter, and it never will.' The apartheid was an environment that dictated where we could go, what we could study, how we could travel, and what we could say. There was no choice and you could feel invisible.

Subjugation invokes feelings of resentment, anger, frustration, and in extreme cases rage. I recognize many of these emotions in myself, which later convinced me to become a monk.

As adults, you become accustomed to feeling powerless and having things dictated to you. Even simple decisions like what movie to watch or where to go out for dinner can become difficult and uncomfortable. You suppress every feeling and emotion you have, and at times become over eager to satisfy everyone around you. Your identity becomes making others around you happy by being overly agreeing. Despite this outward façade of acceptance, the frustration, anger, and resentment of feeling trapped slowly builds up.

As a coping mechanism to subjugation, you will avoid situations in which you may feel constricted. Signing a contract with set terms, committing to meeting people at a specific time and place, going out for dinner; you tend to avoid anything that puts you in a position where you may feel mildly restricted.

The other coping mechanism is surrender. By doing this, you lose every sense of your identity, struggle to recognize who you are, and, most importantly, what could be deemed fair treatment. The feeling of being exploited or taken for granted will never leave you.

If you recognize any of these triggers, it is important for you to know that you can reprogramme this schema. It starts by becoming aware of your thoughts, emotions, and feelings. By acknowledging them, you will start to push away the anger and resentment that accompanies them. *Through mindfulness, you will start to recognize the things that make you happy; and with time, you will develop the courage to voice them with compassion, kindness, and sincerity, as opposed to the anger and rage that you were previously accustomed to.*

5. Mistrust/Abuse

Jennifer was sexually abused repeatedly by a relative when she was six years old. After a few years, when she grew to understand what had happened, she finally mustered up the courage to tell her parents. Her parents dismissed her, making her feel insecure, unsafe, and unworthy of their trust. Years later, the relative still visits their home, which only exacerbates the situation further. Jennifer was later diagnosed with cervical cancer and passed away at the age of nineteen. Having felt so betrayed by her parents, she had little to no faith in anyone who offered help. Mistrust erodes any and all faith in people. In Jennifer's case, the overwhelming feelings of fear and betrayal eventually cost her her life.

Mistrust schema is born from an abusive childhood. The abuse can be emotional, physical or sexual, and **the result is an underlying belief that 'people cannot be trusted.'**

The mistrust trigger makes people constantly wary of being exploited, hurt, humiliated, manipulated, or taken advantage of. They are always suspicious, a state that can easily erode any chance of a healthy relationship. You question the intentions of your loved ones, and often assume the worst. It isn't uncommon to attract partners who only confirm your fears.

There is something unique with the mistrust schema that isn't found in others. In this pattern, the inflicted pain was intentional, by either the parents or the abuser. It is for this reason that the child develops a truly genuine response to a threat that existed. The problem arises when this trigger manifests in adulthood, eroding relationships that are non-threatening and beneficial.

The silver lining is that all of these mental blocks can be challenged and reprogrammed successfully. With mindfulness, you can become aware of the triggers that are sabotaging your relationships. *You can learn to trust again, give more of yourself and cultivate happy, healthy, and loving relationships. All of this is possible. When you develop the courage to resist toxic relationships and no longer tolerate abuse of any form, you are well on your way to healing this schema.*

6. Unrelenting Standards/Perfectionism:

I grew up in an Indian household, and if there is one thing that Indian parents make a top priority it is education. I was the furthest thing from a model student. I loved playing sports which thankfully worked out well for me; but academically, I always felt incompetent. No matter how hard I studied, I was a B-grade student at best. My brothers, on the other hand, were like little Einsteins, excelling in every class year after year. I dreaded the end of every term. I knew my report card was going to be abysmal and that was going to signal the start of a terrible holiday period. One year I came home with my first A-grade pass, expecting a party at home. To my surprise, the only thing I heard was, 'Why didn't you get an A+?' I was infuriated. Nothing I ever did was good enough, and in my mind, it never was going to be good enough.

Perfectionism is associated with unrelenting standards,

often arising from early childhood. Hyper-critical parents can instill in their child's psyche a sense of inadequacy. Because children are so emotionally dependent on their parents, the child feels the need to keep working hard to win their parent's love.

When you have a perfectionism schema, you are extremely harsh on yourself. You set unrealistically high standards and believe that you have to do everything in your power to achieve them. I have seen this schema drive people to become financially successful and famous, but at the detriment of healthy relationships. You have no balance in life, and your health, family, and relationships bear the brunt of this burden. The problem with the perfectionism schema is that you will never feel satisfied, fulfilled, joyous, or happy, because you cannot see beyond your failures.

I have seen those with perfectionism become so paralyzed by the possibility of failure that they avoid starting anything new. Left to their own accord, they will not attempt anything in anticipation of failure – a typical coping mechanism. Some individuals become authoritative leaders so fixated on the success of the project that they lose all concept of empathy for their fellow colleagues and employees.

If you are someone who pushes themselves too hard, cannot pause to enjoy any success, has a fear of starting something new, or believes that your self-worth is linked to your success, you can heal this schema with mindfulness. *Draw your awareness to the patterns that feed this schema. You can slowly challenge these and reprogramme them with time. Healing from perfectionism is possible.*

7. Failure

The failure schema is a subtle variation on the perfectionism and defectiveness patterns. Perfectionism is a sense of feeling like a failure no matter how hard you work. The defectiveness schema is the feeling that 'I am not enough' as a person. **The failure schema is an overwhelming sense of doubt irrespective of how successful you are.** It is linked to one's sense of accomplishment.

The failure schema is born from growing up in an overly critical environment. Parents, friends, siblings, teachers, schoolmates – the constant comparison with other highly successful individuals will give rise to this schema. The emotions associated with the failure schema are anxiousness, sadness, loneliness, a sense of low self-esteem and confidence, unworthiness, feeling inept, untalented and always wanting to be left alone.

Those with failure schema are their own worst enemy. They push themselves extremely hard, and despite any and every success, they will consistently berate themselves. They doubt their achievements, and even when success is indisputable, they credit everything but their own efforts.

Anand was a maverick in the world of healthcare innovation. His company was a leader in diabetes testing, so much so that he was named in the '*Forbes* 40 Under 40' list. Despite this achievement, he constantly felt undeserving of the accolade, incapable of leading the organization, and an imposter in the industry. Anand suffered from a clear failure schema probably triggered by a cluster of other schemas such as deprivation and defectiveness.

Those with failure schema can learn to receive love and recognition. They can become mindful of the negative self-talk that erodes their self-worth, and with time they can learn to see their strengths and talents, and how they contribute to the success of everyone around them. They can learn to see the best in themselves and appreciate their journey.

8. Grandiosity/Entitlement

Brittany was on the brink of divorce when she came to see me. She had grown up in a middle-class family. Her mum was a home executive and her dad served in the army. As an army-kid, you are constantly changing homes and schools, sometimes as often as twice a year. This unstable environment can make it extremely difficult to find love or have any stability in your life. To compensate for the constant moving, her parents gave her everything she ever asked for. She was rarely punished and was never taught to take responsibility for her actions. This gave birth to an entitlement schema.

People with entitlement schema feel so special they believe they can do anything they want. **The rules of life do not apply to them.** An unfortunate repercussion of this schema is a lack of empathy. In Brittany's case, her inability to appreciate, acknowledge, and be grateful to her husband for everything he did erode any emotional intimacy between them.

Entitlement schema can arise from many different situations. A child born into wealth who is given everything his/her heart desires, parents who refuse to set boundaries for their children, emotionally unavailable parents who try to buy their children's love, or children who grew up in traumatic environments – all these could lead to a form of entitlement schema. The core emotion in this schema is a lack of empathy. Those who suffer from it are blatantly inconsiderate to the feelings of others, and sincerely believe that they are superior to others. It isn't uncommon for these individuals to exaggerate their power in an effort to achieve more control or power. Underneath all of this bravado is a feeling of inadequacy. None of this outward display of exuberance can override the sadness, loneliness, and sense of deprivation deep within.

Becoming aware of your negative thoughts, emotions, and actions can help you come to grips with this schema. *Mindfulness can allow you to spot the triggers in your thoughts. You can learn to be more empathetic and aware of the needs of others around you. Healing entitlement could save your relationships and deepen your emotional connection with those around you.*

9. Vulnerability

We all have someone with this schema in our lives, and if they are close to you, their triggers have probably driven you crazy.

The vulnerability schema is associated with a loss of control. The person is so fearful of anything bad happening, they start to catastrophize everything. Simple, ordinary fears are exaggerated and construed to be a mini-disaster.

You would identify a vulnerability schema by an individual's persistent questioning about simple things. They are overly conscientious in an attempt to feel safe.

Fears in this individual can be centred around the fear of catastrophes:

Medical: Illness, heart attack, stroke, cancer

Emotional: Exaggerated anxiousness, fear, obsessiveness

External: Fear of earthquakes, criminals, faulty lifts, natural disasters

Everyone thought Max was simply a hypochondriac. He would get medical tests done randomly every other month to double-check if he was okay. Citing poor family genes as an excuse, he didn't need to be convinced to get more tests or scans done. In a counselling session with Max, we uncovered that his mother was overly concerned about his health. Every sneeze or cough was a reason to see the doctor. This paranoid parenting gave birth to the vulnerability schema in Max. A seed was sown that made him interpret his mother's excessive concern as 'the world is not a safe place.'

There is a fine line between being conscious of certain dangers that may exist and over-analyzing a problem. If you live in a high crime area, it is prudent to get an alarm system. This is normal. Not getting any sleep when a family member is taking a flight can be construed as over-analyzing, especially since there is little you can do when the flight takes off. Healing this schema is possible.

One of the best ways to heal this schema is to use the stoic philosophy of 'challenge your fears.' Write down the worst things that you think can happen. Then try to interpret how bad the outcome will be. Is the worst case as bad as you envisaged? This clarity can help you shift perspective and kick start your healing journey.

Meditation and mindfulness will also be extremely beneficial in helping you scan your thoughts and interpret your fears. The more awareness you bring to these negative thoughts and patterns, the closer you are to healing this schema.

10. Alienation/Social Isolation/Exclusion:

I am a middle child and for the longest time I was convinced I suffered from 'middle child syndrome.' The oldest received the most privileges, and the youngest received the most indulgences, leaving the middle child with an overwhelming feeling of exclusion and isolation. This feeling perfectly describes the exclusion or isolation schema.

The core belief that underpins **the isolation schema is a feeling of not belonging to a group, social clique, friends circle, and, in some cases, family.** Unlike other schemas that are formed in early childhood, isolation is formed when a child is at a more emotionally impressionable age. As a child grows, they develop a need to feel accepted, included, and welcomed. It is the burden of rejection at that impressionable age that triggers this schema. For a child who does not know where they belong in the world, it can be soul crushing.

The coping mechanisms of isolation can vary from avoiding people or situations that may trigger rejection, to outwardly over-compensating with behaviour that makes you stand out. Those who adopt the avoidance technique shy away from groups or any behavioural patterns that may result in them feeling accepted. This coping mechanism only serves to perpetuate their core belief that *'I do not belong here.'*

Those who over-compensate generally make radical changes to their appearance that signal the message, *'I am different, and I do not belong here.'* Their overall emotional disposition is that they do not care for acceptance, even though deep within acceptance is what they want most.

For those who identify with the isolation or exclusion schema, I encourage you to become aware of behavioural patterns that may be reinforcing your core belief. How am I interpreting the signs that tell me 'I do not belong here'? Are there nuanced behavioural changes I can make that allow me to see the world through a new lens? Can I use the Friendship Equation (in 'Circles of Connection') to deepen my emotional connectivity with people? *Isolation schema is often our mind playing games with us. The problem is that our actions follow our thoughts. Using mindfulness and awareness, you can successfully challenge this.*

> *There are eighteen schemas that are grouped into five broad categories called schema domains. The above ten are the most commonly diagnosed schemas. Jeffery Young, the founder of Schema Therapy, describes the key characteristics, coping mechanisms and treatment protocols of each schema in his book,* Reinventing Your Life. *If you are interested in studying more about childhood schemas, I recommend reading* Reinventing

Your Life *by Jeffery Young and Janet Klosko,* Emotional Alchemy *by Tara-Bennett Goleman,* The Handbook of Cognitive Behavioral Therapy *by Keith Dobson,* Schema Therapy *by Jeffery Young and* Disarming the Narcissist *by Wendy Behary.*

Mindfulness and Emotional Healing

The human brain functions in a constant loop between active learning and habitual response. One operates from the pre-frontal cortex (learning) and the other from the basal ganglia (responding). Schemas run from the basal ganglia or subconscious, automatic part of your brain. These programmes will run for an eternity without you even being aware of them. Without even realizing it, you respond and react on the basis of a programme running in the background. However, by becoming mindful of your patterns and triggers, you give yourself the power to reprogramme these schemas.

Schemas are simply behavioural patterns that prevent you from achieving your full potential. Why? Because they distort your reality. Instead of seeing things as they are, we perceive them as we *think* they are.

Mindfulness is critical in healing these schemas. It is a refined form of awareness that allows you to split the narrative from the emotion. You begin to witness subtle emotions, the associated triggers, and their impact on how you react in every situation. You begin to see that the story you have told yourself all these years no longer applies to what you and your life have become.

With mindfulness, you can spot a trigger and identify an emotional coping mechanism. A monk friend always asked his disciples, *'How quiet do you need to be to hear your own voice?'* It was a rhetorical question meant to draw attention to the importance of stillness in one's mind. The quieter your mind, the clearer the picture.

Buddhists say this as well: *'You can see the bottom of a river bed only when the water is still.'* **You can see the depths of your consciousness only if your mind is still.**

Now, with a deepened sense of awareness, draw your attention to the coping mechanisms in your life. Use the schema descriptions above to search for familiarity between your coping mechanisms and possible schemas. The more you investigate, the more clarity you will find. A big clue is often the feelings associated with the schema. In the vulnerability schema, you may not associate with over-protective parents, but the deep fear of losing control is something that you will innately feel. Your intuition will guide you towards the patterns that need healing. **The more mindful awareness you practice, the more precise your pattern recognition becomes.** From noticing the coping mechanisms and emotional triggers, you slowly evolve to take notice of that moment of intention. That is the source from which you can heal a schema. Once you recognize an intention, you can change the lens through which you perceive it. If the thought changes, the action will follow.

In the chapter on strengths 'Start with Your Strengths', I mention the Seinfeld Strategy, which focuses on not breaking the chain. Identify a habit that will contribute to your growth, practice it daily and never break the habitual chain. In emotional healing, there is a chain that has been running for a long time. A chain of subconscious intentions driving maladaptive coping mechanisms. To fully heal we must break the old chain and replace it with a new one. One that will help us discover a happier, more fulfilled Higher Self.

Analyzing Schemas Using the Blueprint Exercise

In the introduction to this book, I pointed out two important realizations:

1. You cannot heal that which you do not understand.
2. You cannot heal that which you are not prepared to change.

Analyzing your schemas and interpreting your lenses are in line with the first realization. The second represents your willingness to heal.

Here is a simple guide to interpreting your schemas

Use the following questions to identify your maladaptive patterns and the associated coping mechanisms.

1. Using the schema descriptions and your Blueprint lenses, can you identify any maladaptive responses in your behaviour?
2. How did your reaction to that situation make you feel?
3. Can you identify your emotional or situational triggers?
4. What is the feeling associated with these triggers?
5. Do any of your Blueprint lenses make you feel the same way?
6. What other situations in your life invoke the same feelings?

7. Can you identify an episode from your childhood that could have given birth to this schema? It may also be a series of environmental stresses at home.
8. If you could respond differently to the situation, how would you have responded?
9. How would you feel if you adopted this new response?
10. When you first notice the maladaptive intention, what can you do to switch to a different response?

The word liberation originates from the Latin word *liberatus* which means to **set free.**

The purpose of this chapter is to liberate you from the maladaptive destructive patterns that are sabotaging your life. By spotlighting the coping mechanisms that are driving your schemas, we have begun your healing journey. The Buddha said, *'Be a light unto yourself.'*

This can be interpreted in many ways. For me, the light represents awareness. By allowing your awareness to shine on the patterns you have developed during the course of your life, you create an opportunity to deepen your insight. These insights are micro-steps in the process of liberating yourself from the stranglehold of your past pain.

A Toolkit for Change

As we move past the midpoint in this book, you are slowly building an arsenal of self-reflective tools. Introspective questions, thought exercises, the Life Blueprint exercise, the interplay with lenses and patterns to help you identify maladaptive schemas. I encourage you to play with these tools. Ask many questions. Be your own scientist.

Question the answers that you have previously accepted as truth.

- *Are your strengths ('Start with Your Strengths') feeding your coping mechanisms ('Freeing Yourself from Destructive Patterns')?*
- *Are certain lenses ('Playing with Perspective') stroking your ego or inhibiting your vulnerability ('Freeing Yourself from Destructive Patterns')?*
- *Is there a relationship between your core values ('Self-love') and your coping mechanisms ('Freeing Yourself from Destructive Patterns')?*

Superimpose your introspective answers with your schemas and lenses. As they say, *the devil is in the details.* Never stop introspecting. When you start to see your emotional and behavioural patterns, your healing journey gets exciting.

Jeffery Young, the founder of Schema Therapy, designed the Young Schema Questionnaire. It is a self-reporting assessment tool that uses 75 items to measure the presence or absence of the eighteen maladaptive schemas at the time of taking the assessment. The questionnaire is available at *www.schematherapy.com*. I encourage you to take the assessment. You may then be able to self-reflect on your lenses and schemas with more clarity.

Healing is a tough, intimate journey that leaves you feeling vulnerable and exposed. For this reason, safety is an essential prerequisite to healing. Most of the thought exercises in this book are self-reflective in nature. Before you embark on them, it is vital that you are in a comfortable safe space, both mentally and physically. If you feel safe and secure, you can explore your vulnerabilities, thoughts, and emotions in a nurturing manner.

I personally love the **Safety Bubble** exercise by Jeffery Young. When you sit down in reflection, imagine a large bubble of safety surrounding you. You can walk in and out of the bubble without damaging it, you can carry into the bubble anything that makes you feel safe and secure, and you can even invite in people who comfort you. It is your safe space. Design it as you see fit, with colours, paintings, trees, plants, furniture, and decorations.

Listen to your favourite music in there. And when you are ready, this bubble can float away to any place your heart desires – on a mountain top, in a forest, on the beach, in a log cabin, perhaps to your favourite city in the world. You can stay there as long as you want.

I use this safe space to reflect on my thoughts and feelings. In the bubble, I am the audience to my feelings. I can explore any emotion or thought in a non-judgmental manner.

One client told me that, from their bubble, they can create other small bubbles that float away from them. In those bubbles, they fill thoughts, emotions, feelings, and behaviours that are not serving their Higher Self. They let them float away.

The next time you sit down in reflection, **why don't you create your own Safety Bubble?**

- How would you design it?
- How do you feel when you are in the bubble?
- Can this be your new safe space?

Having spent more than a decade deeply immersed in spiritual and meditation practices, I have now become a firm advocate of the power of mindfulness in treating pain, schemas, and psychosomatic symptoms. In 1995, a group of researchers used Jon-Kabat Zinn's mindfulness based stress reduction programme in combination with mindfulness based cognitive therapy to prevent relapses in patients with a history of depression. In a post-treatment follow up period of 60 weeks, the percentage of relapses was reduced by more than half. This is testament to the positive impact mindfulness practices can have on one's overall healing.

> *'The only difference between an emotion and its corresponding wisdom is the presence or absence of awareness.'* – Lama Gendun

If you want to heal your maladaptive schemas:

1. Rank your core emotional needs in order of importance. (#5 being the most important)
2. Try to identify maladaptive patterns in your life using schema descriptions.
3. Identify your coping mechanisms.
4. Analyze your schemas in accordance with your blueprint lenses.
5. Cultivate your safe space.
6. Use your 'Tools for Change' to heal your schemas.

SIX

Engineering Your Environment
(Environment, Body, Mind)

Let's start by analyzing one of your environments. It could be your office, your home, your bedroom, your gym, your car, your study, or even your kitchen. Pick any one.

What are five things in this environment that contribute to optimizing your performance, or adding fulfillment to your life?

1.

2.

3.

4.

5.

14 July 2019 was a day like no other in the world of professional tennis. Two old rivals, Roger Federer and Novak Djokovic, fought a gruelling battle that lasted four hours and fifty-seven minutes. It was an epic match for many reasons. Not only was it the longest contested Wimbledon Final in the history of the tournament, but the first Championship to be settled by a final set tie-breaker. Even more remarkable, Djokovic was the first man in seventy-one years to win the Championship from two match points down.

So, what about this spectacular match underscores the importance of your environment?

In a post-match interview, Djokovic said, *'When the crowd is chanting Federer's name, you have to remove yourself from that environment. When the crowd is on your side, it helps. But if you don't have that, you have to find it from within.'*

As the match approached its climax, we saw two equally capable athletes, each drawing strength from two different environments. One, fully absorbing the energy of their external environment, while the other chose to block the external and draw strength from his internal environment.

Is it coincidental that the athlete who went within was the one who emerged victorious?

After two decades of working at the convergence of the physical and mental domains of performance, I have begun to understand the delicate relationship that exists between the external and the internal environments. My approach to optimizing human potential blends both science and spirituality. This dual inspiration has allowed me to discover the intricate balance that exists between the two environments.

For the longest time, I focused primarily on the external environment. In fact, I still spend a considerable amount of time engineering an athlete's external environment for success. However, after spending time in the Buddhist monasteries in Japan, studying Vedic sciences and learning the art of pranayama (breath work) from traditional yogis in the Himalayas, my perspective has shifted. I have come to understand that we are at first strongly influenced by our external environment; and then, through mindfulness, we can cultivate the ability to rise above the trappings of our external environment. Eventually, with years of practice, we can master the art of mindful awareness. This deep state of awareness is so potent that those who attain it have the power to influence (or transcend) their environment. In other words, mastery over our internal environment eventually translates into the external.

Success in any field is directly correlated to an individual's relationship with their environment. Athletes in a state of flow are tuning into their internal environment while navigating the challenges of their external environment. Motivational speakers on stage draw energy from the thousands of guests in the audience, thus utilizing their external environment. Pranayama (breath work) experts who can meditate in icy cold temperatures for hours use the power of their internal environment to block out the external environment. In the pursuit of excellence, understanding the balance between the two is essential.

In this chapter we will explore both the **external** (part one) and the **internal** (part two) environments. The external environment encompasses everything that is tangible. I will give you examples of how athletes, monks, and business executives design their external physical environments for success and fulfillment. The internal environment involves the cultivation of mind (internal) over matter (external). The internal environment (self), when nurtured mindfully, allows an individual to be guided by their innate intuitive wisdom. When you are guided by this wisdom, you are operating from your Higher Self. From here, your contentment and bliss are no longer dictated by your external environment.

In part one:

- How athletes design their environment for success
- The constituents of the external environment
- Adapting to your external environment

In part two:

- The five states of the mind by Patanjali
- The relationship between your internal and external environment
- How to understand and strengthen your internal environment

PART ONE

James Clear, author of *Atomic Habits,* says, *'Motivation is overvalued. Environments often matter more.'* This is a great place to start. Why? Because in the world of sport, the external environment plays a powerful role in an athlete's success. I wouldn't go as far as saying 'motivation is overvalued.' Rather, I would say that the environment in itself is a kind of motivator.

As a sports scientist and an ultra-marathon runner, I was always drawn to the tiny Kenyan village, Iten, that sits on the escarpment overlooking the African Rift Valley. The overhanging archway that welcomes visitors to the village reads **Home of the Champions**, a claim that could not be truer. Fellow sports scientist and author of *The Sports Gene,* David Epstein, called this village *'the greatest concentration of elite athletic talent, ever, in any sport, anywhere in the world.'* At the time of printing this book, four of the five fastest marathon times in the history of the sport belong to Kenyans who train at this village.

This unique running community has single-handedly produced more middle- and long-distance champions than any other city or country in the world.

Iten is a sports researcher's heaven. For decades, scientists, journalists, authors, doctors, and academics have travelled there to understand its secret to success. Everything from muscle physiology, and biomechanics to nutrition, geographical location, training methodology, and socio-economics has been researched. The truth is, very little of the research has been conclusive in crediting any single factor for the village's overwhelming dominance in the sport. If you find this hard to believe, a trip to Iten will put all your reservations to rest. The simplicity of their lifestyle is beyond comprehension, especially in light of their achievements. Growing up in modern cities, our idea of excellence often presupposes the necessity of certain lifestyle pre-requisites. Iten shatters those assumptions.

In Iten, life is as simple as you can imagine. There is a single paved road that runs through the village, with only a few street lamps scattered over its distance. This is why most of the running happens between dawn and dusk. There is no airport, reputable hotel, or big chain supermarket to speak of. As a local resident of Iten, your heroes are the runners. This is why it is so easy to imagine how the next rising star could be the unassuming boy or girl around the corner. Running is in their blood and that is what makes them great.

But this isn't a story about running. This is a story about a community.

In 2006, two New Zealanders who aspired to become the best professional runners in the world packed their bags and moved to Iten. Twin brothers, Jake and Zane Robertson, believed that training among the best and living their lifestyle would have given them a chance to achieve their dreams. The townspeople doubted Jake and Zane would last even a few months. More than ten years later, this is very much their home. When I met them in Iten, it was heart-warming to see that they are as much local heroes as Wilson Kipsang, Eluid Kipchode, Dennis Kimeto, Mary Keitany, and the other legends of the running world.

In 2015, eight years after moving to Iten, Zane Robertson

ran a 59 minutes 47 seconds race at the Marugame Half Marathon in Kagame, Japan. This made him only the fourth non-African runner to finish this distance in under an hour. Brother Colm O'Connell, affectionately known as the *Godfather of Kenyan Running,* said that Jake and Zane Robertson's success is testament to how *'living in an athletic culture or environment, even though you are genetically not belonging to the culture or environment, can significantly impact your life.'*

I've been going back and forth to Iten for many years and if there is one thing that stands out, it is the Kenyan training philosophy – **Good People Make People Great.** If you find the best and get them together, that ecosystem will cultivate excellence. The running community in Iten isn't just supremely talented or genetically gifted. They have an insatiable hunger for success and are prepared to do whatever it takes to get it. Jake and Zane Robertson aren't the only ones who have benefited from this environment. 'The Home of Champions' has become the training hub to almost every runner who has professional aspirations. Why do they all go there? The evidence is unquestionable. Whoever trains in Iten, gets faster.

At the pinnacle of sport, the margin for error is miniscule and the penalty for failure is massive. In an effort to close the gap between strategy and execution (where the margin of error lies), sporting organizations create High Performance Training Centres – environments that are designed to cultivate excellence. A High Performance Centre is an athlete-focused, coach-led, performance-driven system that is designed with cutting edge innovation, science, and medicine. Almost every sporting nation in the world would have one if not a few High Performance Centres in their country. These centres are instrumental in cultivating excellence. They produce talent because the best athletes are invited to work alongside the best coaches, often in a state-of-the-art facility. **When engineering the perfect ecosystem for excellence, it is critical that the 'best of the best' come together.**

Countries like the United States, United Kingdom, South Africa, Sweden, and Australia boast High Performance Centres that are a cut above the rest. In India, I have worked in strength training facilities for professional athletes that have little to no equipment. In Kenya, their High Performance Centre is nothing more than the best runners in the country, coming together and pushing each other. There are no gyms or recovery pools, no testing equipment or fancy eating facilities. Just people - *Good People Who Make People Great.*

In the case of the Kenyan marathon runners, their external environment is their strong sense of community, coupled with immense camaraderie, and driven by a larger purpose. In the cultivation of excellence, does community outweigh facilities? It's difficult to say, but the silver lining is, wherever you are in the world, and whatever your resources, you can design your external environment for success.

Nature versus Nurture

In the making of a champion athlete, the influence of nature (genes) versus nurture (external environment) has been a matter of intense debate, both theoretically and practically, for more than a century. Even without any evidence-based knowledge, one can safely presume there are innumerable components that contribute to moulding a champion. However, the scientific attempt to study the effects of nature and nurture has provided some interesting insights. Over two centuries of empirical and experimental research have tipped the nature versus nurture debate in favour of nature. While the impact of training and the environment cannot be understated, genetic potential is a prerequisite to elite performance. In a nutshell, **elite athletes are built in an environment provided they have the innate genetic potential.**

However, I approached this piece of research a little differently. For me, both nature and nurture are a part of the external environment. Remember, everything tangible constitutes the external environment. The community in Iten, your body, the food you eat, where you train, who you speak too, the car you drive, and so on, are all a part of an external environment that can be designed to optimize your performance. Having the presence of specific genes that predispose you to better athletic performance does not guarantee that you will become an athlete. There are a million prerequisite steps that need to occur for a gene to be expressed. Even with the presence of special athletic genes, the need to design your external environment to allow maximum gene expression is imperative.

At this point, you are probably a little unclear about the components that make up the external environment, and understandably so. I've already mentioned communities, training facilities, food, the body, and crowd support. This obviously isn't an exhaustive list.

As we say in professional sport: **understanding something helps us measure it, and if you can measure it, you can improve it.** So, let us focus on the components that constitute the external environment.

Environments by Design

'We are surrounded by environments. Everything you can see, hear, smell, taste and touch is an environment that is either adding energy to your life or draining energy from your life.' These are the words of Jim Bunch, the founder of 'The Ultimate Game of Life'. Jim conceptualized the **Nine Environments that Make Up Your Life**, which takes the nature versus nurture debate to a level deeper. According to Jim, everything that you interact with, twenty-four hours a day, seven days a week, is a part of your environment. When I first stumbled upon Jim's concept, I was floored by its genius. Not because I did not consider the impact of these components on performance. We are always looking into each of them; but sometimes, in looking at the bigger picture, we inevitably turn a blind eye to some of the more nuanced components that play an integral role in performance enhancement.

Jim's list gives us tangible check-points that we can measure on a daily or weekly basis. As Galileo says, *'Measure what is measurable, and make measurable what is not.'*

Jim Bunch's Nine Environments are:

1. **Physical:** Where you live, where you work, the clothes you wear and the devices/technology you use.
2. **Body:** Your overall physical well-being, the food you eat, your hygiene, your fitness levels.
3. **Memetics:** The information you consume through books, podcasts, films and websites.
4. **Spiritual**: Beyond meditation, breath work, and mindfulness, this component refers to your level of empathy for those around you.
5. **Financial:** Your bank accounts, investments, and things that can help secure you financially.
6. **Relationships:** The quality of your interactions with people you surround yourself with.
7. **Network:** This is an extension of your relationships, but in particular, they represent the tribes, communities, and social networks you engage with.
8. **Nature:** The environment you interact with on a daily basis. Your outdoor ecosystem, your geography – macro (country, city) and micro (street, garden).
9. **Self:** Everything that defines you (feelings, values, strengths, weaknesses, personality, emotions). The self is the ninth environment in the external that transmutes into the internal. I will address the self from an internal environment lens in Part Two.

You must have probably noticed how subtle the differences are between some of these micro-environments.

At first glance, it may appear as though Jim is repeating a lot, but that only serves to highlight the interconnectivity among our environments. When I first studied these micro-environments, I challenged myself: **Am I optimizing my environment for success or trying to optimize myself in my default environment?** In professional sport, designing the environment is imperative. Your environment must work for you. Otherwise your environment becomes an obstacle, something you must overcome. When this happens, you are swimming against the current.

Throughout the book, I highlight the importance of new habit formation in becoming a better version of yourself. New habits can be developed by reprogramming your subconscious mind through the conscious repetition of an activity. Most of us struggle to cultivate a new habit because we are trying to do something new in an old environment.

The old environment is your comfort zone; and trying to reprogramme a new habit within the comfort zone is incredibly difficult if not impossible.

Which brings me to another significant realization:

Realization #8

You cannot heal yourself in the same environment that caused you pain.

To cultivate a new habit, you have two options: you can either rely on your will power to drive you or design your environment to help you achieve it.

Let's say you are someone who wants to wake up at

sunrise to meditate. In your current environment, you may need to set an alarm and then rely on your will power to get out of bed. Engineering your environment for success could entail switching from black-out blinds to slightly translucent curtains that allow the morning sunlight in. This small redesign of your environment will help resync your circadian rhythm to the rising sun, and before you realize it, waking up will no longer be a chore. **When you start to think about your environment as an extension of who you are, success is no more a matter of 'if it will happen' but rather 'when it will happen'.**

Designing your environment to work for you requires mindfulness and awareness. First, you must identify what you would like to achieve. This is your vision board. I generally encourage people to break down their vision or goals into macro, meso and micro[1] goals.

Macro goals are your long-term goals that may take you between one to two years to achieve. I wouldn't recommend having such elaborate goals that you cannot envision them materializing within two years. Besides being extremely difficult to remain motivated for that long, you are also evolving as a person. In two years, these goals may not be as important, or they may have changed.

Meso goals are medium-term goal that may take you between three to six months to achieve. They are broken up into weekly and monthly goals or targets that help you stay focused and allows you to assess your progress.

Micro goals are tiny habits and immediate objectives that, when stacked up over time, help you achieve your meso and macro goals. These are the most important. This is where your focus should be.

When you think about designing your environment, you need to have your micro goals in mind. Constantly ask yourself: **What are the changes I can make within my environment that support my growth or make it easier to remain focused on the micro tasks?**

As a rule of thumb, if you are going to redesign your external environment, start with changes that are measurable. Remember, as Jim Bunch says, that each environment impacts the next; so a positive change in one should bring about a positive change in another.

The DIY (Do It Yourself) Guide to Optimizing Your Environment

As promised, I am going to walk you through a few small changes you could make to each of the nine environments or in your lifestyle. I use many of these techniques with my professional athletes and corporate executives. I would recommend you pick a few that are relatively inexpensive and start with those. Once you start to notice the impact of these, you will be motivated to spend a little more time, energy, and resources optimizing your external environment.

1. Physical Environment:

1. Switch your blackout blinds to translucent curtains. They will help you wake up with the rising sun. (If your room is near a streetlight that filters into your room, do not change to translucent curtains.)
2. Clean the air filters in your air conditioner and use air purifiers at night. Dust pollutants can impact sleep.

3. Keep the room at 19/20 degrees Celsius at night. Cooler temperatures promote better sleep.
4. Switch to a standing desk at work. If you are sitting, you can swap your chair for a Swiss Ball. The ball improves your core stability and the constant movement is healthy for the spine.
5. Change your light switches to dimmers. Lighting impacts the production of melatonin. Dimmers help control your exposure to harmful light.
6. If you are exposed to street noise, change your windows to double glazed, noise-blocking glass. If you travel in public transport, carry noise-cancelling headphones. Ambient noise is one of the biggest undercutters of happiness.
7. Avoid tight, restrictive clothing which impedes blood flow.
8. Keep a Balance/Wobble Board in your office. Besides improving your stability, they improve the neural conductivity between the foot and the brain.
9. Cover the LED lights on your television, electrical chargers, and devices with black tape. Research indicates that LED light exposure significantly impacts sleep quality.
10. Spend twenty minutes a day walking barefoot. It grounds your energy, is rejuvenating, and stimulates the acupressure points on your feet. Preferably do this in nature.

2. Body:

1. Cold showers in the morning and evening help reduce inflammation. If you cannot have a cold shower, try a hot/cold contrast shower (20 seconds cold, 10 seconds warm x 10 cycles)
2. Switch your vegetable oils to cold-pressed oils. Vegetable oil is the biggest contributor to inflammation in the body.
3. Deep tissue massages once a week stimulate collagen production and increase the flexibility of the myelin sheath (myofascial massage).
4. Super slow training reduces the risk of injury and increases strength development.
5. Adding theanine to your black coffee balances the neurotransmitters in the brain, prevents telomere depletion, and promotes better sleep.
6. Deep breathing exercises (Pranayama) stimulate the vagus nerve which promotes relaxation, reduces inflammation, improves memory and the neural conductivity between the gut and the brain.
7. Keep a red-light lamp in your bedroom. Exposure to red-light at night enhances your deep sleep patterns.
8. Limit your intake of aged, smoked, or cured foods. They have a high histamine content, which causes headaches, anxiety, and sleep disorders.
9. Drink Yerba Mate (indigenous to South America). It improves mood, lowers cholesterol, reduces inflammation, and balances your blood sugar.
10. Thirty seconds of high intensity exercise before every meal improves your body's glycemic response.

3. Memetics:

1. Download audio books and podcasts. The content files are lighter, and you can listen to them while training or travelling.
2. Watch a new TED talk once a week.
3. Improve your information absorption by writing down key points while you are listening to a podcast or audio book.
4. Subscribe to an online journaling app that allows you to document your learnings digitally.
5. Teach something new to someone every week. This is called the Feynman Technique, and is designed to help you identify the gaps in learning.

4. Spiritual:

1. Download a meditation app like Calm, Headspace, or Insight Timer. They have guided meditations that will help you cultivate a mindfulness practice.
2. Join a spiritual organization or find a spiritual mentor you resonate with.
3. Align with a non-profit organization through which you can volunteer your time and services.
4. Start journaling your thoughts and emotions. There should be a minimum of three entries a week.
5. Use TDSC **(Transcranial Direct Current Stimulation)** to improve your memory, ability to focus, and coordination. In the past ten years, research has proven that mild electrical stimulation is safe and without any known side effects.

5. Financial:

1. Conduct a StrengthFinder Assessment (start with your strengths) to understand the key strengths you can leverage to become financially stable.
2. Set up fortnightly, mandatory meetings with your financial advisor. Take responsibility of your money.
3. Diversify your investment portfolio, but not without guidance from a qualified friend or financial consultant.
4. Set financial goals and define the micro and meso steps that will allow you to achieve them.
5. Create a monthly budget and checklist of your expenses and try hard to stick to them.

6. Relationships:

1. Use the Concentric Circles of Friendship from the chapter, 'Circles of Connection', to categorize your relationships. This makes it significantly easier to manage your time and energy.
2. Practice being emotionally present when someone speaks to you. This is the secret to effective communication.
3. Find a mentor who can guide you. Remember, you can find mentors in different areas of well-being (physical, spiritual, financial, mental, technical, social).
4. Use the Art of Subtlety as given in the chapter, 'Being Mindful in Communication and Conflict', to emotionally detoxify yourself and prevent burnout.
5. Practice being vulnerable with your intimate circle of friends.

7. Networks:

1. Identify three of your 'core' interests, and then search for online or offline groups and communities that share them.
2. Use them to push yourself out of your 'comfort zone'.
3. If you are passionate about a subject or a cause, create your own group in your locality. The excitement of watching it grow will also motivate you.
4. Challenge yourself to introduce one new member to the group or community every six months.
5. Diarize the meetings for up to three months. Build the community into your lifestyle, and emotionally commit to be a part of it.

8. Nature:

1. Map out all the parks, gardens, running paths, beaches, lakes, and outdoor meditation gardens within five kilometers from your home and office.
2. Commit to spending twenty minutes, three times a week in nature.
3. Create a green corner in your office. Preferably with real plants, foliage, or trees.
4. Use fresher scent aromatherapy diffusers in your home and office.
5. Plan one holiday a year in nature. Use this time to re-reconnect with Mother Earth and ground your energy.

9. Self:

1. Use a few online psychometric tools to better understand your personality type. Many of the tools in this book will also help you understand yourself. Knowing the type of person that you are is the first step to becoming the person you want to be.
2. Commit to understanding and healing old childhood trauma. The chapters 'Playing with Perspective' and 'Freeing Yourself from Destructive Patterns' are a great place to begin this journey. You are a result of your subconscious programmes. It is important for you to know that you can rewrite these programmes.
3. Commit to a daily practice that helps you centre yourself. Yoga, journaling, meditation, breath work, and sitting in silence are wonderful practices to explore.
4. Self-confession on paper has immense healing power. Write down any negative thoughts, emotions, and feelings – and then burn the paper. This is a powerful healing ritual.
5. Practice gratitude to those who have hurt you. This is a very difficult exercise, but it will help you heal your pain and shift your energy. The pain they may have caused you has, in fact, contributed to your growth. If we see this pain as an opportunity for growth, we immediately transcend the hurt. This is where you find your Higher Self.

These basic guidelines for each environment are only a starting point in your personal journey of growth. The purpose of life is to evolve into a better version of yourself. Because we are significantly affected by our environment, we must become mindful of the environment we create.

Spirituality teaches us that we are a part of the whole. Each of the nine environments is part of the whole. We may feel like we are experiencing a higher degree of success in one domain as compared to another, but because all parts are interconnected, success becomes interconnected too. Use this reality to improve your life. Improvements in some domains will be easier. Use them as much as you can. Be mindful of the other domains but do not fight the initial resistance in the other areas. Embrace them and with time they will all merge organically.

The OODA Loop

In 2009, during the Japan Open ATP Tennis Tournament, I was introduced to the concept of *kaizen*, which means 'change for better.' Masaaki Imai, author of the book *Kaizen: The Key to Japan's Competitive Success*, credited the kaizen philosophy as the key to Japan's systematic approach to business improvement. The word has now become a metaphor for a mindset that represents **'continuous incremental improvement.'** What started off as a pure management concept has now evolved into a life philosophy.

Since then I have adopted this notion in my work with professional athletes. In elite sport, the environment is constantly changing. Success hinges on our ability to adapt to an ever-changing environment. The pace at which our ecosystem evolves isn't unique to sport. In the military, the term used for an environment that is impossible to predict and always shifting is VUCA. VUCA stands for Volatile, Uncertain, Complex and Ambiguous.

Just like in the military, an athlete's ability to adapt to a world prone to sudden change is the differential between winning and losing.

United States, Air Force Colonel John Boyd conceptualized a related theory that is applicable in a fast-changing environment. He called it the **OODA Loop**, which stands for: Observe, Orient, Decide, and Act.

In the OODA Loop, you first gather data using your senses and perception (observe). Then you process that data into a single coherent framework that gives you workable options (orient). Step three is to choose the best course of action (decide), and step four is to act swiftly and decisively.

The OODA Loop has helped me in two ways:

- With my athletes who need to act decisively, it highlighted the importance of gathering data as a prerequisite to good decision making.
- With clients and patients who operated with less urgency, it forced them to make a decision.

This OODA Loop is an Infinity Loop ('Playing with Perspective') unto itself. Our actions change our environment. With every change, a potentially new set of variables comes into play. This immediately takes us back to step one, where we must once again observe the environment and gather data. Those who are most successful in war, sport, and business are often those who can cycle through this loop quickly and efficiently, allowing them to nimbly adapt to a fluid, ever-changing environment (which in turn relates to our previous point about the importance of embracing dynamic balance).

Physical environments differ from situation to situation, person to person. Occasionally, you may have the luxury of time in engineering your environment for success. If this is the case, be mindfully aware of everything you introduce into your environment. If you are in the military, a sportsperson, or work in situations with a high degree of uncertainty, your ability to assess your environment and adapt to it is critical. In my opinion, this skill is best honed through practical knowledge and on-ground experience.

In the beginning of this chapter, I introduced two environments: the internal and the external. Over the course of part one, we have explored many of the variables that play a role in designing our external environment. I hope that I have given you the insight necessary to mindfully make changes to your external environment that align with your greater goals and purposes.

Now that you understand the role your external environment plays in your success; I want to turn the lens inward. As you have noticed, the external environment is complex and laden with many challenges, often beyond our control. Such is the nature of the external environment. In your pursuit of excellence, just as it was for Djokovic, there will come a time when your external environment does not provide the support you need to overcome a challenge. That does not mean it is the end of the road.

It means you need to find an alternate source of motivation. That source is within you. It is your internal environment, and commonly known as the Higher Self.

Spirituality has taught me the pathway to the Higher Self. It is a reservoir of pure energy that is always available to you. When you access this energy source, the external environment will no longer exclusively dictate your success.

PART TWO

My time as a monk initially led me down the path of religion. A decade later, I can intellectually borrow the essence of many religious scriptures in the cultivation of a deeper spiritual practice. In fact, my spiritual practice, together with my study of the Vedic sciences, has provided me with the tools that are pivotal in my approach to both performance and healing. One Vedic scripture that has transformed my thinking is the *Yoga Sutras* by Patanjali.

Patanjali was an Indian sage who is credited as the author of the famous *Yoga Sutras*, a collection of 196 aphorisms, divided into four chapters. In the Western world, he is recognized as the 'Father of Yoga' for his classification of yoga known as Ashtanga (eight limbs of yoga). It is one of the most complete works examining the relationship between the spirit (purusha) and matter (prakriti). That is, the relationship between our spiritual beings and our physical existence.

In the *Yoga Sutras*, Patanjali describes the 'five states of the mind'. Each state encompasses a level of awareness regarding the thoughts and emotions that flow through your mind. These states of awareness are directly correlated to how you interact with your external environment.

'Your life is a projection of your state of mind', Patanjali says. In other words, our mental state is the cornerstone for all personal growth. When I began my in-depth exploration into the five states, the relationship between our internal (self) and external environments became crystal clear. More importantly, the need to cultivate the internal environment took centre stage.

Let us take a closer look into Patanjali's five states of the mind:

1. **Ksipta:** This is the lowest state of mind. In ksipta, the mind is unable to fully comprehend its thoughts and experiences. It jumps from one object to another without being able to focus on anything. As a result, the mind is restless, anxious, confused and cannot understand or relate peacefully to the true nature of any object, thought, or experience. This state of mind is not conducive to growth because there is no control over the mind and its senses. A person will alternate between extreme states: love and hate, like and dislike, pain and pleasure, boredom and enthusiasm. Even basic mundane activities are challenging for a *kspita* state of mind because all decision-making and cognitive abilities are compromised.

   This mental state is perpetuated by a cycle of unhealthy eating patterns, substance abuse, lack of physical exercise, negative self-talk, and toxic relationships.

2. **Mudha:** This is a dull state of mind. An individual in this state is aware of the need for change but lacks focus and intent. As a result, they are held back by a lack of energy and vitality. There are brief moments of motivation that channel some of their energy towards vices that only satisfy the senses. However, their efforts rarely ever yield results due to an inability to focus and concentrate on the task at hand. Consistent disappointments create an overwhelming feeling of sadness, depression, entrapment, anxiety, and a deep sense of unworthiness.

This mental state is perpetuated by poor lifestyle choices, an unhealthy family environment, the lack of positive role models, low self-esteem and a lack of financial resources.

3. **Vikspita:** This is the butterfly mind. In the first two states, the mind is distracted and unaware of its Higher Self. In the Vikspita state, the mind alternates between moments of clarity and distraction. Even though the mind is restless, it is fully aware of its Higher Self. Through the cultivation of spiritual practices, the mind is able to experience a sense of calm, bliss, happiness, tranquility, and contentment. However, because the mind is restless, the resultant effect of these practices is often short lived.

   This mental state is easily recognizable through one's lifestyle. The individual is mindful of their spiritual practices, the food they eat, the importance of quality movement, and the need to be surrounded with people who stimulate them intellectually and raise their vibrational energy. They are unable to sustain this yogic lifestyle for prolonged periods of time, but despite falling into a distracted state of mind, their awareness of a Higher Self allows them to return to practices that support their spiritual growth.

4. **Ekagra:** This is a concentrated or single-pointed mind. In this state, the mind is fully focused and aware and can hold its attention on a single point without being affected by any external factors. During this state, all inner chatter, confusion, restlessness and agitation subsides. The mind

is calm, relaxed, and has clarity. Ancient yogis describe this state as the starting point of one's spiritual journey. This is the place where the ego dissolves, intuitiveness is awakened, and one's perception of the world is no longer restricted to the five senses. You are in absolute control of your thoughts, emotions, and feelings. This mental state is recognizable by one's heightened level of awareness, clarity of thought, awakened intuition and the desire to disassociate the self from itself.

5. **Niruddha:** This is an arrested or fully focused mind. In this state, the individual is able to hold their awareness on a single point of focus for as long as they desire. No thoughts, feelings, or emotions, can distract this state of mind. There is complete stillness in the mind, which does not react to life's ever-changing situations. This is the pathway to enlightenment and liberation.

   This mental state is recognizable by one's overall aura of contentment, grace, and tranquility. A person in this state is fully present and absorbed in every moment to which they give their attention. Those in the Niruddha state have a contagious aura. In their presence, you will experience their level of bliss, contentment, and calmness. Unfortunately, the average person cannot hold this exalted state of being by themselves.

Allow me a disclaimer. It took me a long time to understand and interpret the five states of mind. So, if you are a little confused, that's perfectly okay. Try to read the descriptions a few more times. If you only grasp the level of awareness associated with each state of mind, that is all you need to move ahead.

The teachings of Patanjali are profound. I was drawn to them because modern psychology is limited when it comes to understanding the relationship between our internal environment and the external environment. For me, the **five states of mind beautifully articulate the relationship and impact between an individual's level of awareness and their external environment.**

Have you ever read something that intuitively felt so right (because you may have probably experienced it so many times) and you could not understand what the fuss was all about? When you start to understand the five states of mind, it will feel like that.

A child is deeply affected when a friend stops speaking to them. A professional at work is stressed when a volatile market impacts business, while their colleague isn't troubled at all. These are examples of individuals in different states of mind. Over the course of our lives, we experience different individuals in different states, and often we witness how they are shaped by their environment. Sometimes those effects spill over onto us as well. These are examples of how the lower states of mind are directly impacted by the external environment.

A monk who has been practicing mindfulness for years and isn't afflicted when diagnosed with a chronic disease. An athlete who can block out the noise in a stadium and focus on the task at hand. These are some examples of how the higher states of mind (states associated with a stronger internal environment) can block out the external environment.

This might make more sense if I walk you through each state of the 'five states of mind' (internal environment) and explain how depth of awareness correlates to the external environment.

The first two states of mind, **Kspita** and **Mudha**, describe individuals strongly shaped by their environment. Because they cannot hold their awareness to a single thought or activity long enough, their ability to make positive decisions that create personal growth is severely compromised. People in the *Kspita and Mudha* state have no interest in cultivating their Higher Self and are often removed from any experience or environment that could foster personal growth.

The third state, **Vikspita**, describes an individual unable to stay fixated on the processes that develop their internal environment. They can be easily influenced by the external environment, but fortunately for them, they are mindful enough to choose their environments wisely. Through practices like meditation, they are aware of their ability to remove themselves from the stress of their external environment; but once the meditation practice ends, they may start to feel the burden of the situation again. With practice, they can hold a higher vibrational state for longer.

The fourth state, **Ekagra**, describes an individual who can transcend their environment. When in meditation or fully focused, the external environment has no effect on their state of mind. Athletes in a flow state are in *Ekagra*. Their conscious and subconscious minds are in sync, and when navigating their external environment, they are completely unaffected by any hurdle they may encounter. In this state, you transition from being influenced by your external environment to your external environment having little to no effect on you.

In a remote Buddhist monastery in Northern India is a group of monks who are practitioners of the ancient science of Pranayama (the practice of breath control). These monks use a breath work technique called *Tum-mo* to regulate their core body temperature. In temperatures well below five degrees Celsius, these monks sit in meditation, draped only in wet sheets. Using their ability to raise their core body temperature, they can dry these sheets in under an hour of meditation. *'It is a profound example of the mind's ability to influence the body'*, says Dr Herbert Benson, Associate Professor of Medicine at Harvard University. These Buddhist monks first detach themselves from the cold external environment, and subsequently influence their environment. They are an example of someone in the Ekagra mental state.

The fifth state, **Niruddha**, describes individuals with the capacity to influence their environment. These individuals have mastered the art of controlling their internal environment. Their level of internal awareness is so heightened that their vibrational energy can shape their environment. This state is achieved by very few self-realized souls. Prophets and spiritually awakened gurus would fall in this category.

Channeling Your Energy

In part one of this chapter, we focused purely on the impact of designing our external environment. I have always said that if an intervention can help a professional athlete get a 0.1 per cent performance gain, it can potentially help an individual in a more pronounced way.

We know that designing the external environment for success is a must.

The purpose of part two of this chapter was to shift your mindset. Using the 'five states of mind', I wanted to establish the importance of our internal environment. Will most of us ever get to a stage where we can influence our environment (niruddha)? It is highly improbable, but not absolutely impossible.

Will a mindfulness practice that develops our internal environment help us optimize our performance and lead to greater fulfillment in life? YES. As Michel de Montaigne says, *'The greatest thing in the world is to know how to belong to oneself.'*

Part two of this chapter was never about discounting the importance of the external environment. Neither was it about making you a monk. It was about showing you how, through mindfulness and the development of your internal environment, you can get to a stage of life where your troubles and circumstances don't trouble you anymore.

In With The New

Living as a monk, I was taught that *'You are a projection of your mind.'* **Mindfulness is simply the process through**

which self-mastery is achieved. It is a process that requires unwavering discipline. The result of which is a sense of freedom. When the mind is free to explore the depths of its consciousness, the true journey of self-discovery begins.

In the five states of the mind, we learn that true bliss, tranquility, peace, and harmony are achieved by mastering one's internal environment. That journey of self-mastery is so elusive, legend has it that those who attain this state are given the benediction of sacred knowledge. The Indian sage Valmiki who performed meditation for thousands of years was blessed with the knowledge of the Ramayana. Siddhartha Gautama became the Buddha through the process of meditation and self-realization.

In sport, athletes use visualization techniques, meditation, NLP (neuro-linguistic programming), breath work, and a host of other tools to master their minds. Those who master these techniques are inevitably those who succeed in the long run. We now see a host of professional athletes (Kobe Bryant, LeBron James, Kerri Walsh, Virat Kohli, Derek Jeter) advocate for meditation. In the world of entrepreneurship, Silicon Valley founders are rapidly becoming spokespeople for practices that cultivate your internal environment. Apps like Headspace and Calm that teach meditation have garnered valuations worth billions of dollars.

The world is finally awakening to the realization that the internal environment is as important to your success as your external environment.

Two Sides of the Coin

After two decades of training professional athletes, if you asked me for one rule to live by, it would be this: **Learn from your successes.**

This book is about decoding the functionality of the human brain, then using it to understand and enhance your life. I have heard the phrase *learn from your failure* more than a million times in my life. This is the thing about failure. When you fail, your brain is so fixated on the result that it will dissect the entire experience in search of all the tiny errors you made. Most people are unable to see and appreciate the small successes and valuable lessons learned even in a supposed 'failure' or setback.

When you learn from your successes, you can interpret each positive step that contributed to the win. These tiny, positive markers are your blueprints for success.

Success leaves you many clues, if you are willing to look for them.

Why am I saying this to you? There are thousands of examples of individuals who have achieved mind-blowing success by focusing purely on their external environment.

Then there are those who took a chance and optimized their internal environment as well.

- Is the big difference in the amount of wealth they accumulated? Probably not.
- Is there a difference in the quality of their journey to that point? Definitely, yes.

Here is how you can develop your internal environment:

1. Practice a basic Box Breathing Technique for twenty minutes daily.
2. Sit in solitude for twenty minutes daily. Use this time to reflect on your thoughts, emotions, and feelings. Explore each of these with the audience lens.
3. Sleep and wake up at the same time each day.
4. Hydrate and eat as much clean organic vegetables as possible.
5. Keep a Gratitude Journal.
6. Practice spreading kindness and compassion throughout the day.
7. Practice the Art of Subtlety (as in the chapter, 'Being Mindful in Communication and Conflict')

We began this chapter with a question. What are five things in your environment that contribute to optimizing your performance?

- In closing this chapter, let's reflect on your answers.
- How many of your answers reflect changes in your external environment?
- Were you aware of the impact your internal environment has on your external?
- If you could rewrite your list, would it change and if yes, how?
- Rank your five environmental changes in order of priority.
- How would you design your environment for success?

If you want to optimize your environments:

1. Break your long-term goals into micro habits.
2. Identify which of Jim's 9 Environments they apply to.
3. How can you design your environment for success?
4. Identify your mental state and the pathway to mental liberation.
5. Start your journey of inner engineering.

SEVEN

Being Mindful in Communication and Conflict (Mind, Relationships)

What are the five emotions you experience the most? In order of strength (1-weakest; 5-strongest) rank each of the emotions you frequently feel.

1.

2.

3.

4.

5.

Next, I want you to think of a friend or colleague who for an extended period was upset with you. It could be a current situation in your life, or something from the past. Recall the memory of the incident that fractured that relationship. Absorb it.

Now, try to recall the attempts you made to heal that friendship. Travel back in time to those moments. How were your attempts received? How did you feel when your friend brushed off your efforts to communicate with them?

How often have you wished you had an opportunity to explain the situation from your perspective? Perhaps, you were sure that if you had that chance, your friend would understand, and all would be forgiven.

There is a good chance you are right about that.

Finally, I want you to think of a friend you have been angry with for many months, perhaps even years. Think of every attempt that *they* made to reach out to you. The emails, calls, messages, texts, coffee requests. How many times did you turn away their attempt to heal your relationship?

Here is the Paradox of Communication:

We often do not give others the benefit of the doubt we wish for ourselves.

Before you continue reading this chapter, I want you to absorb this truth. How would life be different if you extended the 'olive branch' first?

According to quantum mechanics, we are all matter and energy, and all energy is interconnected. If we are indeed connected, **our ability to communicate is the most**

important skill in life. One could argue that our survival depends on it.

Is our ability to communicate limited to the five senses? Dr J. B. Rhine, a botanist who founded the parapsychology lab at Duke University, suspected that humans are capable of communicating and perceiving on other planes. He coined the term ESP (extrasensory perception) to denote ways we are able to gain information not perceived through the traditional five senses (which is why some people refer to ESP as the 'sixth sense'). Although his original ESP experiments at Duke were never duplicated, the field of parapsychology that he helped launch has continued to explore modes of perception we generally classify under the umbrella term **intuition**. I too, remain convinced humans are able to transcend the five senses, even if we haven't yet been able to scientifically document how this occurs.

In this chapter, we will explore:

1. The science of effective communication
2. The types of conflict that exist
3. A few key communication strategies
4. The Art of Subtlety – the art of emotionally detoxifying yourself and cultivating happier and healthier relationships

Components of Effective Communication

Have you ever wondered why we take for granted one of the most important skills needed for our survival and happiness? You learnt a language in school and studied the principles of composition. Maybe you also studied rhetoric or participated in debate club. Beyond that, how have you cultivated your ability to better understand and communicate with those around you? I have met people who can speak half a dozen different languages but are still terrible at communication. Just think for a moment. Is it possible that our entire framework of communication is flawed? Is Dr Rhine correct? **Could our languages, our words, and our reliance on the five senses limit our quest to feel and communicate effectively?**

In the face of conflict, most people are able to perceive their communication shortcomings to some extent; yet in most cases they lack the tools to assess the situation and execute the best course of action. On its face, communication appears to be a simple process between two people: one who initiates a conversation (speaker) and the other who responds (listener). Within this seemingly simple equation, there is endless complexity and potential for missteps, often exacerbated by our own egos.

Earlier in the book (in 'Circles of Connection'), I spoke of Dr Lester Luborsky's Core Conflict Theory, which states that all individuals want to be understood, empathized with, seen, valued, respected, and treated fairly. Irrespective of the nature of the relationship, if these values are absent or compromised, a relationship will struggle to exist in harmony.

Why is this important in a chapter on communication? Simple. Effective communication is the key to a healthy relationship. **The deeper the connectivity between**

the speaker and the listener, the stronger the bond of intimacy. If connectivity is absent, conflict will arise. The only thing standing between conflict and intimacy is communication.

In *The Seven Habits of Highly Effective People*, Stephen Covey summarizes in one line the key to effective interpersonal communication: **Seek to understand, then to be understood.**

A simple yet incredibly profound statement. The first half of his statement emphasizes the importance of being a mindful listener. I once heard a monk ask some disciples, *'Are you listening to understand or are you listening to respond?'* In Luborsky's Conflict Theory, the four components (understood, valued, seen, and respected) are consequences of being a good listener.

Listening has many dimensions to it. We have all encountered people who seem to be listening, but just aren't emotionally present. Then there are those who pretend to listen. Probably the worst are those who listen selectively, with the key agenda of the conversation being their response. None of these is an effective listening technique.

Being emotionally present in a conversation is a product of the conscious mind and a skill that needs to be cultivated. When you develop this skill, you learn to be empathetic towards the other. Without even saying a word, the other person feels your presence.

Your emotional presence is your skin in the game. That is the reason why they say effective communication is 90 per cent listening.

The second part of Covey's statement emphasizes the importance of responding mindfully.

Doing so addresses all of the necessary values in Luborsky's theory. It is only after a mindful response that the other person is sure we have truly listened to them: that we understand, see, and empathize with them; that we value and respect them; that they can trust us to treat them fairly. A mindful response is the fruit that grows in the soil of active listening.

You do not have to be a therapist to understand the power of empathetic listening and response. In the chapter on maladaptive schemas, we saw the impact of parents not being mindful in their relationships with their children. We have all been in a situation where our words fall on deaf ears. Take a moment and try to recall one of those incidents in your life. The sense of hollowness, loneliness, and unworthiness you felt was probably overwhelming. In some cases, you may have felt worse after that interaction.

Here is the scary thing: often, these disappointing interactions involve someone close to you, someone who loves you. *Failing to be emotionally present in a conversation is not tied to love or the lack of it. You may love the person with all your heart, but if you are distracted and not fully present, they will pick up on that.*

Hidden Perceptions

Cleve Backster was a counter-intelligence and interrogation expert for the US Army, and in 1948 he founded the CIA's polygraph (lie detector) programme. He later taught lie detection to the NY Police Department and the FBI. But in 1966 he stumbled upon a rather remarkable discovery.

One evening, he connected the electrodes of his polygraph to a leaf of a dracaena plant. A polygraph uses weak electrical currents to measure slight surges in human emotion through sensors. When he initially poured water into the plant, the machine did not indicate a strong response. Backster knew that the most effective way to trigger a reaction strong enough to register on the polygraph is to threaten an individual's well-being, so he decided he would burn the leaf of the plant that was connected to the electrode. Even before he had a chance to light a match, he noticed a dramatic upward surge on the polygraph. When Backster left the room and returned with matches, he noticed another upward shift on the polygraph, evidently caused by his determination to go ahead with this threat. To take the experiment forward, Backster began to reluctantly burn the leaf of the plant, which produced a much weaker reaction. When he simply pretended that he was going to burn the leaf, there was no reaction.

Backster concluded that plants have the ability to differentiate between a real and perceived threat. Moreover, he suspected all life has a kind of consciousness – what he called a **'primary perceptual skill'** – at the cellular level. *'I think Western science exaggerates the role of the brain in consciousness,'* he said in an interview. *'Whole books have been written on the consciousness of the atom. Consciousness might exist on an entirely different level.'*

Backster became obsessed with this line of inquiry. Although the mainstream scientific community was skeptical about his conclusions, his work inspired books like *The Secret Life of Plants* and *What Plants Know*.

What does this have to do with the subject of this chapter? If indeed we have certain extrasensory perceptive capacity at the cellular level and a deep innate ability to detect the intent of another, this has profound implications for human communication.

It would help explain why so often we are terrible communicators. It would explain why we seem to have a sixth sense that can detect the sincerity of another. When we sense they are not emotionally present, their words carry little impact. In other words, **in the absence of authentic emotional presence, all our other communication skills, all our gifts with words, amount to nothing.**

Mindfulness can change all of this. In mindful meditation, you draw all your awareness to a single point, your breath, and hold it there. In mindful communication, that single point becomes the other person: not just what they are saying, but their entire being. If we can at the same time remain mindfully aware of ourselves, all our thoughts and emotions come into the purview of awareness. We see things as they are and not as we wish them to be. We are in a position to feel, interpret, think, and act in a manner that is appropriate and helpful.

In professional sport, being mindful and perceptive is the norm rather than the exception.

I remember my early days in cricket. We had a saying, **'Character over cover drives.'** Teams would rather choose an individual we know is going to fight for the team over someone who is exceptionally talented but selfish. Great athletes have their own sixth sense: an ability to tell who can be trusted in the heat of battle. In team sports, poor communicators make for poor performers in the long run, especially in contact sports. Why?

In contact team sports, if the miniscule margin for error can put you in a potentially life-threatening situation, communication is no longer a luxury; it is a necessity.

No 'I' in Team

In team sports, the coach or captain has to safely manage multiple egos, keeping in mind the vision of the team. If a player has only one per cent of value to add to a set-up, it is my job as the leader to create an environment that allows us to leverage that one per cent. As in any organization, getting team members to work together is the secret to success. In sport, we do not have the luxury of time. We need to be super efficient communicators. It is the only way we can fast-track trust and accountability within a system.

In *The Art of War,* Sun Tzu highlights the importance of trust in any battle. **When you trust the person next to you, you can channel your energy towards an external threat.** If your energy is focused on the person next to you, you leave yourself exposed and vulnerable to attack from the outside. The best teams in the world harbour trust and create platforms that bridge the gap between people. In sports and war, you cannot afford failures of communication. The penalty for error is simply too high.

The focus of this chapter is on interpersonal communication, and having spent almost two decades in team sports, I thought it would be helpful to break down the essentials of healthy team communication. **These principles apply to any team environment, including the workplace.** Moreover, the same dynamics are at play in building one-on-one camaraderie and rapport:

1. Punctuality is essential. It shows respect for every member of the team. Respect is the foundation upon which all other values are built.
2. Integrity: If it is wrong, do not do it. If it is false, do not say it. Nothing erodes the core values of an organization more than dishonesty.
3. The team environment is not a platform for politics, religion, or discrimination (age, gender, race, socio-economics). In this space, everyone is equal.
4. Respect the facilities. Keep them clean and in good working order. It shows respect to the individual who will use them after you.
5. Create a culture of learning. If everyone is contributing to the growth of the organization, there is inherent respect. Learning develops organizational culture and builds communication skills.
6. Have a clear organizational structure and job description. This makes it easy for individuals to know how to address their grievances.

Decoding Conflict

Is it safe to say that conflict is inevitable? Even monks in a monastery, who spend a lifetime mastering mindfulness, sometimes find themselves in a position of conflict. The question is not whether conflict is universal, but why we consider this a bad thing. Just as we must learn to be grateful for every experience (good and bad) that made us who we are, we should learn to appreciate the lessons that conflict can teach us. To put it in two words: **conflict clarifies**.

As an entrepreneur, I find myself in conflict positions on a weekly basis. The younger generations do not hesitate to voice their opinions; and their comfort level in challenging me has contributed greatly to my growth. **Conflict helps me grow because it tests my perspective and my assumptions.**

Monkhood taught me a great deal about how to approach conflict. First and foremost, I listen – and resist the temptation to immediately respond. I allow the other person to finish, knowing that if they feel they have the chance to fully express themselves, only then will we have a real chance at dialogue. I am also extremely mindful of their tone, body language, and emotions. If they are angry or upset, I request time to think before I respond. *Mindfulness hasn't necessarily removed conflict from my life; instead, each conflict is now an avenue for constructive growth.*

There are three types of conflicts: task conflict, relationship conflict, and value conflict.

Task Conflict: This is often a workplace conflict that rises from the management or expectations around a certain task.

Relationship Conflict: This can apply to both workplace conflict and personal conflict, and often arises from contrasting personalities, and the particular chemistry between people.

Values Conflict: This conflict arises from a fundamental difference in core values (as described in the chapters 'Self-love' and 'Circles of Connection') and limiting beliefs. Most relationships end because of a conflict of this type.

Let's try a little thought exercise:

- Can you identify the type of conflict that arises most often in your life? Is it task, relationship, or value conflict?
- How often do you find yourself in these conflict situations?
- Is it generally with the same person or group?
- Does the narrative of these conflicts have a common theme(s) or set of emotions?
- Would your approach to the situation change if you viewed it from another perspective?
- Have you been fair to the other person? Have you effectively listened to everything they have to say?
- What could you change to ensure this situation does not repeat itself?
- Can you communicate your willingness to change with a tone of sincerity and compassion?
- What do you think is the lesson you need to learn from this conflict?

With mindfulness, you can transform a highly stressful conflict situation into an opportunity for personal growth, and for building stronger relationships. The above questions are simply tools to open your mind to a whole new world of perspectives and possibilities.

Embracing Conflict

Our aversion to conflict is one of the biggest ironies in life. We all aspire for growth in every aspect of our lives, and one of the best ways to grow is to be pushed outside your comfort zone. As Tony Robbins says, *'All growth starts at the end of your comfort zone.'* And very often it is through conflict that we are pushed beyond our comfort zone. It is ironic because we want to evolve; yet we fear the process that pushes us towards evolution.

In the chapter 'Self-love', we had the realization:

You cannot love yourself if you hate the experiences that have made you the person you are.

Here is a companion realization:

Realization #9

You cannot evolve if you fear the process of growth.

I will never forget what happened to me in Kimberley, a little town in the Northern Cape of South Africa (and best known for the De Beers Diamond Mines), where I was working as a High Performance Coach to a professional cricket team. In my early days in professional sport, I was known to be a 'taskmaster': the one who physically pushed his athletes beyond anything they could have imagined. Everyone knew and feared the day I would 'throw down the gauntlet.' This was a day I would set a physical challenge so difficult that, if you achieved it, you would walk away thinking 'anything is possible'. That was the idea: to shatter every limiting belief you had about your potential. This was the day you met the best version of yourself.

On one particular day, an exceptionally talented young fast bowler was going to take on the gauntlet. It was a simple running exercise that theoretically could be completed in six and a half minutes. However, it was so physically taxing that it generally took hours. This young man took his talent for granted. I knew that he was on the brink of making the national team, but his attitude towards work held him back. After fifteen minutes he picked up his shoes and started walking away. 'I didn't sign up to run. I am a bowler and if you want me, you know where to find me,' he said.

I pulled him aside. That afternoon (it has happened only a few times in my life) I became a person I didn't recognize. I was loud, aggressive, and angry. I pulled him back and ran him into the ground. Four hours later, he was still trying to complete the exercise. But I refused to let go. Like a dog with a bone, I was unrelenting.

He eventually finished it in just under eight hours. A week later he came through with a career-best performance. 'Thank you,' he said to me after the match. 'After what you put me through, nothing on a cricket field will ever feel tough.'

The times I had to transform myself into a person I was not especially proud of always involved a player of exceptional talent. They were so good that they were their own worst enemies. Pushing these people out of their comfort zone often seemed like an insurmountable task. The need to push them forced me to take extreme measures.

This taught me an important lesson. **Knowing who you are is vitally important. Knowing the type of person that can push you out of your comfort zone is just as important.**

The more you evolve, the tougher it will become to find these people. People who understand you, communicate with you, and trust you enough to say and do what they need to, to help you redefine your upper limits.

Sometimes the communication we need is gentle and compassionate. At other times, we need conflict and confrontation. Both can be healthy forms of communication, and both are essential to our growth.

Approaching Conflict with Mindfulness

Why are monks so happy and content? While some of it has to do with the cultivation of their inner environment, it also has to do with the fact that they often operate in silos, removed from any potential relationship conflict.

For most of us, conflict is an inevitable part of our lives, especially if you have aspirations of growth – spiritually and materialistically. The challenge arises in what Aristotle beautifully observed: *'To be angry with the right person, in the right way, at the right time, and for the right reason.'*

Through mindfulness, and a cultivated and heightened sense of self-awareness, you can perceive the situation and its associated emotions with clarity, focus, and calm. Instead of operating from a place of disdain, anger or defensiveness, you will be able to trust your intuition and approach each situation with compassion and an open mind.

There are five ways in which you can approach a conflict. Each style will determine your communication method. Not all are conducive to growth. But by practicing mindfulness, you can choose an approach that is authentic, sensitive, produces physical and emotional stability, and has a positive effect on the relationship.

Here are the five ways to approach conflict (**The Thomas Kilmann Conflict Model**):

Style	Resultant Effect
Competing	Win/Lose
Compromising	Lose/Lose
Accommodating	Lose/Win
Avoiding	Lose/Lose
Collaborating	Win/Win

Competing: When one individual has a goal in mind and isn't prepared to stop until they achieve it. This becomes a battle of resources (energy, money, time) and often, while one person emerges victorious, the relationship is eventually strained.

Compromising: In this situation, everyone sacrifices something in an effort to find harmony. While it is highly effective under time constraints, it is never a long-term solution. It is important to ensure the compromise is fair, and mutually agreed upon. Communication in this situation is vitally important and will determine if there is going to be any further engagement. This is a lose/lose situation because both parties sacrifice some of their needs. However, a compromise could be the springboard to a potentially wonderful relationship, if the communication is honest, transparent, and fair.

Accommodating: In this situation, the material outcome is not as important as the process. For one or both parties, maintaining harmony and sanctity in the relationship is more important than winning an argument or any potential materialistic benefit.

Avoiding: In this situation, both parties steer clear of the potential conflict for one of three reasons: the conflict is meaningless, you don't have the time to manage the situation, or you are not sure how you feel about the situation. It is a stop-gap solution that generally prevents emotions from escalating out of hand.

Collaborating: A win/win situation is always the best outcome one can hope for. In any win/win situation, all parties approach the situation with an open mind, ready to explore and try out different possibilities that could serve each individual's best interests.

I wish picking a communication style was as easy as reading a few paragraphs and then mindfully making a choice. Unfortunately, **just like schemas, your communication style is a programme that runs in your subconscious mind.** All too often, you may only later become aware of how your own communication style affected a given situation. This does not mean this programme cannot be changed. It just requires mindfulness and practice.

Here are a few self-reflective questions you can ask when you find yourself in a conflict situation.

The answers to these questions will help you cultivate a more refined awareness – one that makes you mindful of how you respond in every situation.

1. How much do I value the other person?
2. How familiar am I with the entire situation?
3. Do I have the necessary time and energy to deal with the situation now?
4. What am I thinking and feeling right now?
5. Is resolving this conflict a priority?
6. Could there be a potential middle ground in the resolution?
7. Do I understand the consequences of any action I am considering?
8. Can I communicate my thoughts with kindness?

My Only Rule in Relationship Conflict

As a result of my work with subconscious schemas and emotions, I find myself mediating relationship conflict more often than I would like. This involves the whole gamut of relationships: friends, lovers, parents, children, siblings, co-workers, teammates. I have spent countless hours guiding people through the process of understanding their emotions and navigating potential hurdles, all in an effort to find a harmonious solution. All of this has taught me a few things:

1. In conflict, people tend to forget the good times they have shared together.
2. As a result, they act in a manner that is either unbecoming of them or erodes the respect and love that once existed.
3. In times of conflict, people need to be reminded to act with compassion.
4. What they later regret the most is the manner in which they spoke to each other during the counselling or mediation process.

Taking all of this into account, I give couples one rule to adhere to: **You are allowed to argue or fight, but not to scream at each other.**

In life we often learn most from the nasty experiences. Again, conflict teaches, conflict clarifies. How we approach conflict, how we conduct ourselves in the heat of the moment is critical. Mediating hundreds of nasty experiences has taught me that screaming in rage or **anger is the quickest way to erode the dignity of a relationship**. Buddhism teaches us that everything is in a state of impermanence. No matter how bad the situation is, it too shall pass. What becomes harder to evolve from is the sense of emptiness you feel after someone you once loved disrespects you.

A Play with Words

A few years ago, I was in a relationship that felt like hard work every second of the day. I remember telling my partner, 'I feel extremely incompetent. No matter how hard I try, I am constantly disappointing you.'

Even though everything seemed to be falling apart, her sense of humour was intact. She would tell me, 'As long as you know that you are the problem, we have a chance of figuring it out.'

In a lightbulb moment, I designed **a thought exercise** to gauge our level of alignment. I had to figure out if I was crazy or if we simply weren't on the same page.

We each took a piece of paper and wrote down three adjectives that best describe each of the following words: relationship, love, and marriage. It was such a simple but revealing exercise. Everything was suddenly crystal clear.

I described a relationship as intimacy, companionship, and trust. She described a relationship as safety, family, and loyalty. When we looked at the other's answers, we were both taken aback. For her, a relationship had to culminate in a family or marriage. For me, it was more about trusting that we were there for each other and being mindful enough to deeply immerse into every moment.

I have started using this simple exercise in most of my relationship counselling and team-building exercises. Seneca said that we use the word 'friends' too loosely. This exercise showed me that we use far too many words loosely.

Why don't you try this exercise with a partner, lover, friend, or business colleague?

You can describe a few 'anchoring' words that exist in the relationship. Here is a sample list to choose from: **friendship, loyalty, love, teamwork, relationship, support, happiness, security, intimacy, marriage.**

When you compare notes, you can immediately gauge the degree of alignment between both individuals by looking at the themes that define the relationship. It is very simple. **Differences in perspectives are one of the biggest contributors to conflict.** This exercise puts a spotlight on how differing perspectives on a single word can lead to conflict.

To take the exercise further, you can even superimpose these notes with your core values (as discussed in 'Self-love') to determine if the gap can be potentially bridged. The more information you have, the better equipped you are to be an effective communicator.

Mastering Nuanced Communication

Effective communication is an art and a skill. Like all skills, it improves with practice. Unfortunately, most of us dedicate little time to mastering a skill so essential to our success, productivity, and growth, and to the quality of our relationships. As a therapist, I witness relationship hurdles almost every day. Very often, the mismatch in communication is the gap between our intent and our communication. This gap can be bridged if you keep two things in mind:

1) command over different communication techniques, and
2) a deep understanding of what you would like to communicate.

I am going to take you through **five easy communication techniques,** but I cannot stress the importance of being mindful and emotionally present during all your interactions. As we discussed earlier, humans have a remarkable ability to pick up communication on other planes (whether you call this intuition or a sixth sense). This is a super power that can help you connect and communicate better than you ever imagined. It all starts with mindfulness.

1. **Mirroring:** Researchers Atzil, Hendler, and Feldman found that social synchrony (commonly known as mirroring) is important for bond formation and adequate social functioning. Mirroring is when you subtly mimic the body language or choice of words used by the other person. Mirroring allows us to demonstrate trust, empathy, respect and rapport. The secret to mirroring is that it has to be subtle and natural; otherwise it appears forced and inauthentic.

2. **Reading Body Language:** We have all been in an argument where one person says, 'It's not what you say, it's just how you are.' In other words, often our body language communicates far more than our words. Understanding body language can give you insights into how comfortable someone is in a relationship. You do not have to be an expert but knowing a few simple signs could help immensely.

   Signs that someone is comfortable: The individual moving closer to you, or leaning towards you, they turn their body to face you, a slight head tilt, a genuine smile, subconscious physical touch, their head resting on their hand.

   Signs that someone is uncomfortable: The individual touches or rubs their face or neck, they cross their arms, they point their feet away, they turn away from you, or they avoid eye contact.

3. **Open-ended Questions:** In his TEDx Talk, Mike Vaughan, author of *The Thinking Effect*, says that when you teach people *what* to think, you restrict their ability to think and grow. When you teach someone *how* to think, you cultivate their ability to adapt to different situations. After studying numerous top performers, Vaughan found that high achievers challenge the unknown by phrasing questions to open a world of new possibilities. In a nutshell, instead of close-ended questions that limited possibilities, top performers ask open-ended questions that elicit deep thought.

   Here are some open-ended questions you can use to enhance your interpersonal relationships:

   - How can we deepen the emotional intimacy in our relationship?
   - What can I do to make you feel respected and valued?
   - How can we explore ways to bring back the 'wow' factor in our relationship?
   - What could we do to support each other more?
   - How can we change our physical space to create a comfortable environment for us?

4. **For Your Eyes Only:** In my corporate workshops, I invite individuals to pair up and spend a few minutes gazing into the others' eyes. Your eyes are the windows to your soul. When you look into someone's eyes, the connection is subtle yet deep and powerful. This exercise may initially make you slightly uncomfortable. You may laugh, smile, talk, look away, all in an attempt to distract the other person or avoid the vulnerability of the exercise. We do

this because when someone looks into your eyes, you feel as though they can see everything about you. When you stay with this experience, you slowly break down those inhibitions, and with time allow for a deeper level of connectivity.

To foster deeper relationships, connect to the individual by looking at their eyes, especially when they are speaking about things that are important to them. Eye contact is also a fabulous way to ensure you are emotionally present and mindful.

5. **Embrace Vulnerability:** *'If we live behind a mask we can impress, but we can't connect'*, says Donald Miller, CEO of StoryBrand.

   In their work, Brené Brown, Shasta Nelson, Adam Grant, and Robert Cialdini address the power of vulnerability in establishing deep, strong emotional connections. The evidence is overwhelming. To truly foster meaningful friendships and relationships, we must communicate from a place of emotional vulnerability. On a recent speaking tour in India, I told the audience, *'If you truly want to connect with someone, you have to leave a piece of yourself with them.'* The more sacred the piece of yourself you share, the higher the probability of a truly deep, emotional connection.

The Art of Subtlety

The Latin origin of the word *subtle* and *subtlety* means 'finely woven' and was used to describe fabric. In the realm of communication, subtlety is the quality of being understated, delicate, or nuanced. In describing the subtlety of an argument, we make reference to the fine weave of the words and thoughts used to convey a certain meaning or message.

Before I elaborate on this concept of subtlety, I want to bring your attention to the definition and metaphorical reference of the word *suspension.*

Suspension is the act of stopping something from happening or operating. It is a word used across multiple fields. In chemistry, certain substances have a suspension state (chalk in water); in architecture, bridges are built using suspension cables; and in employment, you can place an employee on suspension. When something is held in a certain state for a prolonged period of time, we refer to it as being in a state of suspension.

On both the physiological and psychological levels, a state of suspension can have incredible benefits, but also potentially disastrous ramifications.

Pranayama is the Vedic practice of breath control, commonly used by yoga practitioners. It is a mindfulness practice that draws one's attention to the rhythmic cycles of inhalation and exhalation. *Prana* means breath or life giving force, and *yamah* refers to the suspension of that breath. Within the practice of *pranayama*, there is a component called *kumbhaka* which involves the retention (holding) of breath. Antara kumbhaka is holding your breath with air inside your lungs, and Bahya kumbhaka refers to holding your breath without air inside your lungs.

When you practice pranayama, you realize that the power

of the practice is not in the inhalation or exhalation of the breath – it is in the suspension state between the cycles of inhalations and exhalations.

Similarly, in healing from emotional pain, our ability to hold an emotion helps determine our ability to understand, acknowledge, appreciate, and transition from that pain. If we allow pain to become anger, and anger to become resentment, we will not be able to process the core of the pain. **Only when we are mindful enough to hold an emotional state will we find the power to heal it**.

Breath retention beyond a certain point, of course, will cause asphyxiation. In the same way, holding on to emotional pain for a prolonged period will also have a disastrous impact on your ability to function. Suspension states have incredible power up to a point; beyond that, they can be life-threatening.

A patient, Bernard, once called me sounding highly stressed. He was in an emotionally abusive relationship and it had reached a breaking point. The situation with his live-in girlfriend was toxic and sensitive, and Bernard was desperate for physical and emotional space. I asked him, 'How did the situation become so toxic so quickly?' He replied, 'It has always been like this, but I have reached a point where I cannot keep quiet anymore. I am tired of walking around on eggshells. I have no voice and I am afraid if I say something, it is going to trigger another pattern of rage in her.'

Employees frustrated at work, parents tolerating verbal or emotional abuse from their teenage children, live-in couples silencing their voices to avoid conflict, lovers withholding the resentment of a lack of intimacy in the relationship, are all examples of toxic relationships compounded by a lack of emotional connectivity and communication.

The **Art of Subtlety** is the solution to preventing such toxicity. I discovered this strategy during a stint with the cricket team Kings XI Punjab, during the Indian Premier League (IPL) season. The IPL is a high stress sporting environment, and rightfully so. Held once a year, this competition is the hallmark event in cricketing circles – it is an opportunity to truly make your mark on a global stage. Anyone who does well over these forty-eight days is guaranteed to have a dramatic life shift after the event.

Every high stress environment carries its own set of problems. At the IPL, I had to deal with cricketers who were not getting an opportunity to play; those who did get an opportunity but could not perform; coaches who weren't able to select the teams they wanted; and youngsters petrified of letting their team down. Among all of these were a few exceptionally talented cricketers who were just there to make money and contributed nothing to overall team culture. The result of all of this was a proverbial 'pressure cooker' environment, which if not managed properly could become highly toxic.

Emotional toxicity comes from holding on to emotions for longer than is needed to understand, acknowledge, and process them. Emotional toxicity can be found in every environment, and very often is the result of a given personality type, as opposed to a situational trigger. A person who holds on to a negative emotion at work will also do so in their personal relationships. It is a subconscious pattern that they need to become mindfully aware of.

Subtlety is a mindfulness technique to address emotional toxicity at its core. It is a two-fold technique.

- First, I encourage individuals to understand, acknowledge, process, and release the emotions they are feeling in a situation, *precisely at that moment*. Doing so seems simple, but it can be an enormous challenge. We tend to do anything to avoid, deflect, or delay dealing with powerful emotions. The idea behind this technique is to avoid emotional build-up, either negative or positive. Subtlety is a kind of emotional detoxification.
- Second, the expression of our emotions in the moment must be understated, delicate, and nuanced. This is a critical but a difficult aspect of the Art of Subtlety. The emotions we feel in a given situation may be intense and powerful. It is possible to overwhelm the other person with the intensity of these emotions. To be *understated, delicate, and nuanced* is a show of courtesy and consideration for the other person. It is mindfully responding in a way that they can hear and absorb; that doesn't put them on the defensive; and that accounts for their feelings as well.

It is just as easy to overwhelm *ourselves* with our own emotions. When we exercise restraint in expressing these emotions, we are also exhibiting humility. By not getting lost in the power of our own emotions, we remain present to the other person, and to the larger situation. We do not allow the experience of our emotions, or our expression of them, to become self-indulgent. In emotionally challenging moments, you might think back to the 'Actor/Audience technique'. Even though you are an actor in the important scenes of your life, you must occasionally step back and be a non-judgmental witness.

How could Bernard have used the Art of Subtlety in his relationship?

Subtlety does not only pertain to negative emotions. In fact, positive emotions are better suited for laying the foundation for this practice.

Whenever Bernard felt grateful for anything his partner did to acknowledge him or make him feel comfortable, he could have said, 'I don't say this enough, but I appreciate the small things you do for us.' When he felt emotionally strangled by the way she reacted, he could have said, 'I understand and respect that you are unhappy with the outcome of the situation. Right now, I want to help, but I need you to please help me feel comfortable enough to speak my mind. I am fully committed to finding a solution.'

Subtlety is delicate. **The Art of Subtlety has a few incredibly powerful benefits:**

1. It forces you to be more mindful in every conversation and interaction.
2. It forces you to understand and process the emotions you are feeling at that time.
3. It gives you the freedom to express how you feel in that moment, in a gentle, nuanced manner.
4. Expressing yourself in the midst of the situation prevents emotional build-up and allows you to gauge how the person is reacting to your initial thoughts and feelings.
5. The process of emotionally connecting to people with your thoughts and feelings deepens the level of connectivity with them.

Practicing the Art of Subtlety

Think of a few scenarios that you may find yourself in. They do not need to be specific or have any names associated with them. Start by thinking of general situations that could trigger some emotions in you. They could be centred around your work and personal life. Here are a few examples:

1. A colleague wants to work with you. You like them as a person, but you are not quite sure you are ready to work with them.
2. You went home hoping to have a quiet evening, but your partner has invited some guests over without informing you.
3. There is a small family function, but you would prefer to not attend.
4. Your partner surprises you by making one of your favourite meals.
5. Your children are speaking to you and your partner disrespectfully.
6. You expected a piece of work by a certain time, but your team/colleague has not completed it.
7. You want to express your love and appreciation to your parents for everything they have done for you.
8. You partner does not like your friends and it bothers you.
9. You feel like you need to work on the intimacy in your relationship.
10. Your child's latest examination results are amazing (or disappointing).

These are examples of situations we may all find ourselves in. Each could potentially trigger an emotion that pushes you off-centre and affects your interactions with other people. Spend a few minutes thinking about how you might convey your feelings and emotions in the above-mentioned situations in a few simple, subtle sentences.

You can then make your own list of present and future scenarios and articulate your thoughts about them. If you foresee a potential conflict or challenging situation, spend a few minutes thinking about the possible outcomes and how you would like to convey your thoughts and emotions with subtlety.

Subtlety and the Art of Confrontation

At this point, you might think back to my discussion about embracing conflict, and specifically to the story of how I confronted a certain cricket player in order to get him to take his game to the next level. Where is the subtlety there, you might ask. How is this consistent with what I have just been proposing?

Such moments of confrontation that push someone out of their comfort zone are generally few and far between. Getting in someone's face like that is effective only after you have established a foundation of trust – in other words, in the context of mindful communication. Moreover, even in the moment of conflict, you must remain mindful. Your confrontation is not self-indulgent, but strategic and purposeful. You continue to read the other person, gauge their reaction, and adjust your own words and actions as needed.

In other words, subtlety is still relevant in not-so-subtle situations.

We opened the chapter with you listing down five emotions that you experience the most.

- Take some time now to ask yourself how effective you are in communicating these emotions.
- How does your level of effectiveness align with how you have ranked each emotion?
- Can you use the concept of subtlety to express how you feel at that moment?

Spirituality teaches us that there are **two perspectives to every situation or experience: the way it is and the way we think it is.** Buddhism calls these two perspectives the relative truth and the ultimate truth. For each of us, the gap between these two realities is notional. Effective communication is the only way to bridge this gap in interpersonal relationships. At the core of effective communication is mindfulness, the art of being emotionally present in every interaction or experience.

What I admire about the personal growth industry is the acknowledgement that we are not perfect, but we still should not give up on ourselves, regardless of the circumstances, or the pain we have gone through or perhaps are going through. None of this matters. All that is important is the commitment to improvement and growth.

If you want to become an effective communicator:

1. Have faith and trust in your extra-sensory perceptions (intuition)
2. Become a mindful listener and responder
3. Know the type of person who can push you out of your comfort zone
4. Be aware of how you would like to manage conflict (communication strategy)
5. Apply the 'Only Rule in Relationship Conflict'
6. Define key words in your relationship and find your alignment
7. Master nuanced forms of communication
8. Practice the Art of Subtlety

EIGHT

Self-transcendence and the Power of Purpose (Mind, Relationships, Environment)

In this, the final chapter of the book, our first thought exercise is based on the Japanese Philosophy of **Ikigai** (pronounced ee-kee-guy). The word means *'a reason for being'* and encompasses the things that make one's life worthwhile. In communities and cultures that practice Ikigai (by that name or another), purpose becomes the cornerstone of a life well-lived.

Dan Buettner, a reporter with National Geographic, has devoted much of his life to documenting the world's so-called 'Blue Zones' – a handful of regions with an unusually high life expectancy. One of those is Okinawa, a chain of islands in southern Japan. There, Ikigai is the beating heart of their culture. Buettner's own translation for the term is 'a reason to get up in the morning'. Interestingly, another factor contributing to longevity there is that people belong to strong social support networks called **Moai** that often last an entire lifetime. Moai means *'meeting for a common* *purpose'*. **Purpose can be both individual, and shared,** as with the marathon runners of Iten, Kenya.

As a philosophy, Ikigai sits at the confluence of four truths. With deep reflection, self-exploration, and experimentation, you will uncover the values, strengths, and skills that will help you find the balance of Ikigai in your life.

To find your Ikigai, you must answer four questions:

1. What do you love? (Passion)
2. What are you good at? (Profession)
3. What can you be paid for? (Vocation)
4. What does the world need? (Mission)

Defining your Ikigai isn't an overnight process. It can take weeks of reflection, or even longer. However, at this stage of the book, you are already well on your way to understanding and defining your core values, strengths, and skills. We are going to use the Ikigai formula to translate your reflections from the previous chapters into a workable model.

Ikigai is very much a trial-and-error process. Constructing your model is step one. The true test comes when you use your model in the real world. **Is it giving you the sense of happiness and fulfillment it promises?** This is the acid test.

To begin, set aside some time for reflection. Explore the depths of each question. When you bring your answers together on a venn diagram (as above), a vision for your life may start to appear. You are even welcome to create two or three options as a life purpose. Remember, Ikigai is a way of life, and **this tool is merely a compass to guide you in the right direction.** This journey will not be without ups and downs. But as Nietzsche said, *'If you know your "why", you can endure any "how."'*

A Personal Note

Looking back at my life, I can relate to Nietzsche.

Twenty years ago, oppression was so indoctrinated into the sytem in South Africa, it was virtually impossible for a person of colour to dream of a future in sport. For almost every person of colour, the apartheid had cut deep wounds. Adamant that the system had to change, my decision to study Sports Science, was fuelled by a bigger picture, a larger mission: to do my part to make sure no child ever felt the pain of discrimination in sport. I had a single vision. **Make sport an equal opportunity platform, absent of any and all forms of discrimination.**

Why is this narrative important in a chapter on self-transcendence?

Twenty years ago, a system tried to push me out. Armed with only a dream, I chose a path that was off the beaten track. Pushing through the pain, forced to leave home multiple times, tolerating both physical and emotional abuse at every level. At no point was it an easy journey but knowing that my efforts might help a disadvantaged child get the same opportunities as everyone else propelled me forward. This is why I believe in serving a higher cause.

The Science of Self-realization

In this chapter on self-transcendence, I am going to purposely veer away from academic theories and remain grounded in my personal understanding and experience of transcendence. Given how it has played such an integral role in my life, I feel this is the best way to do justice to the subject.

Throughout the chapter, I will narrate personal stories, my learnings from Vedic sciences, and the amazingly powerful life journeys of a few remarkable souls. I hope to unravel the essence of self-transcendence, the factors that lead to it, and a simple process to guide you to your own realizations.

I grew up in a pious home, and even though our resources were sparse, my parents introduced me to the concept of serving humanity very early on in my childhood. We didn't call it service or self-transcendence. We called it **sewa**, a Sanskrit word that means 'selfless service'. Growing up in an Indian home, *sewa* is part and parcel of your daily life. Taking care of elders, helping out families that are less fortunate, doing a bit of service in your local religious organization, donating food and clothes to charities, the list goes on. Sewa can take many shapes and forms, all of which exemplify two principles:

- service is an integral part of who you are; and
- at no point should you expect anything in return.

As my mentor H. H. Radhanath Swami says, *'To the degree we cultivate the spirit of selfless service, to that degree we'll actually find bliss in our lives.'*

As we explore the definition of self-transcendence, you will notice there is very little distinction between self-transcendence and *sewa*. Both are about using your resources (financial, physical, mental, social) to serve a cause greater than yourself.

In the chapter on perspectives, I highlighted the difference between focus and perspective. In the pursuit of self-transcendence, while we are all focused on the same thing, the East and the West approach the subject from completely different perspectives. The differences are cultural and ingrained in how we think about serving humanity. I will leave you to decide which approach works better.

What is Self-transcendence?

Pamela G. Reed wrote an important paper on the subject. Her definition of self-transcendence is:

The capacity to expand self-boundaries intra-personally (toward greater awareness of one's philosophy, values and dreams), inter-personally (to relate to others and to one's environment), temporally (to integrate one's past and future in a way that has meaning for the present), and trans-personally (to connect with dimensions beyond the typical discernible world).

It is an elaborate definition that addresses four domains: intra-personal, inter-personal, temporal, and trans-personal.

Here are four simple questions to help you understand your own capacity for self-transcendence.

1. What are the core values you can cultivate that are in alignment with serving humanity?
2. How are these values empowering you to help those around you?
3. How can you draw on your knowledge and experience to help others?
4. How are your values helping you connect to the Higher source (Universe)?

Self-transcendence is a character or personality trait. While I was familiar with the concept of service through a spiritual lens, it was the Kenyan running community in Iten that truly demonstrated the power of self-transcendence for me. While it is clear that a strong sense of community is a major factor contributing to the success of Iten's runners, books about the Kenyan running phenomenon have devoted little analysis to how they successfully galvanize their community.

When you spend time in Iten and scratch below the surface, you will uncover why this community has thrived so successfully! Every professional runner in Iten who wins a major marathon gives a percentage of their winnings back to the community. These contributions create training camps for kids and young aspiring runners. There, young runners are given accommodation, food, training clothing and shoes, coaching and mental support.

Participants are offered follow-up support by the professional runners for as long as ten years. This relationship isn't without benefit to the professionals as well. Through these camps, they find young talents who push their limits in training, resulting in each athlete constantly redefining their upper limits. The professionals give back because it helps the community maintain their dominance over the sport. One runner told me: *'When you are faced with extremely tough conditions in a race, and you need to dig deep to find inspiration, all you have to do is think about the other runners back in Iten. When you understand how each victory for a Kenyan runner helps the entire community, it's easy to find the strength to push a little harder.'*

In other words, the Kenyan runners are never just running for themselves. They are running for an entire community. Talk about a reason to get up in the morning!

Self-transcendence and the Hierarchy of Needs

In the chapter on environments, I also addressed the importance of cultivating both the external environment and the internal environment. I referred to the internal environment as the 'Higher Self'. Abraham Maslow's **Hierarchy of Needs** sheds some light on why I have done so. In his book *Motivation and Personality*, Maslow suggests that basic needs must be met before an individual has the capacity or desire to serve his secondary or higher-level needs. According to Maslow's hierarchy, our needs are as follows:

- Physiological (air, water, food, sleep, clothing, shelter)
- Safety (personal security, emotional security, health, well-being, financial security)
- Belonging and love (friendship, intimacy, family)
- Esteem (recognition, status, importance and respect from others)
- Self-actualization (realization of one's full potential)

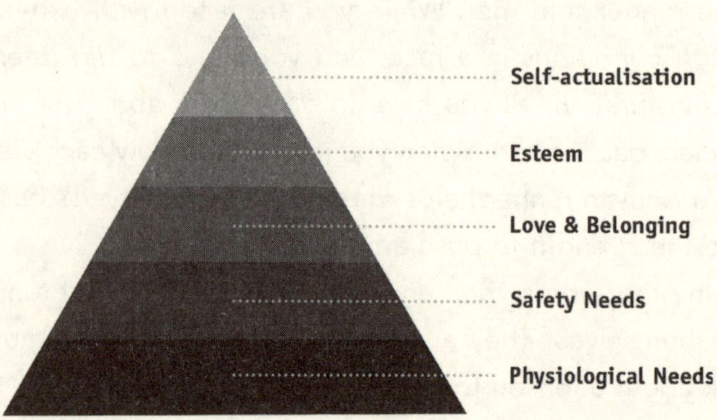

MASLOW'S HIERARCHY OF NEEDS

Is Maslow's hierarchy truly, as some have claimed, Universal?

The Story of Sindhutai Sapkal

In a tiny village district outside Mumbai, a nine-year-old girl, Sindhutai, was forced to marry a man twenty years her senior. Having come from abject poverty, this young girl was forced to quit school after passing grade four. Over the course of the next ten years, she gave birth to three sons. At the age of twenty, and while nine months pregnant, her husband in a fit of rage repeatedly kicked her in her stomach, dragged her out of their home and left her to die in a nearby cowshed. Traumatized by the pain, she passed out and gave birth to a baby girl in the cowshed. Upon waking, Sindhutai realized that she had to cut the umbilical cord herself. Using a stone she found in the cowshed, she cut the cord. Exhausted and helpless, she carried her child for kilometers to her native village, only to be rejected by the villagers there. With no home to call her own, Sindhutai found shelter in the local cremation grounds. It was the only place she could be safe at night. Early each morning, she scavenged through the burial grounds for food left behind. During the day, she walked the railway platforms begging for food to feed her child.

One day, Sindutai was sitting under a tree, contemplating her life. The burden of her daily struggle had become too much to bear. The only thing holding her back was the fear of her child's safety. When she looked up, she noticed that the small patch of shade she was sitting in was provided by a branch that had been completely hacked. She thought to herself, *How amazing is the branch? Even in the state that it is, it is still merciful and considerate enough to provide me shade.*

The following day while walking on the railway platform, she heard a baby cry. It was a newborn resting in the arms of its mother who had passed away. She picked up the baby and made numerous attempts to seek help from the authorities, but they all refused aid.

She recalled asking God, 'In this state that I am, unable to even look after myself or my child, how is it that you see me fit to look after another soul?' At this moment, her thoughts were drawn to the tree branch that was hacked but still mercifully gave shade to others.

From that moment on, Sindhutai vowed to adopt any orphan child she encountered. As the numbers grew, she began to beg for more. Not only did she want to provide food, but also shelter and a good education to each child.

Sindhutai has been serving orphan children in India for fifty years now. She is affectionately known as the 'Mother of Orphans'. She has transformed the lives of more than 1500 children, many of whom have become doctors, academics and lawyers. She has 282 sons-in-law, 48 daughters-in-law, and more than a thousand grandchildren. After many years, the husband who kicked her in her stomach turned homeless and destitute. Out of the kindness in her heart, she forgave him and accepted him as well, not as her husband, but as one of her children.

Sindhutai Sapkal was honoured by the President of India with the Nari Shakti Award – the country's highest civilian award dedicated for women. She has won more than 273 awards for her dedication and work in child services.

Her life exemplifies how, **when you find the courage to serve humanity selflessly, you find yourself. It is through purpose that you discover the strength you never knew you had.**

Achievement versus Fulfillment

Like millions of others in India, Sindhutai had virtually no stability in the lower levels of Maslow's pyramid – the basic human needs he presumes must be met before we aspire to the higher level of self-actualization. Yet, this did not stop her from serving humanity. She did not patiently work her way up each rung of his hierarchy. In a sense, she moved straight to the top. Her moment of realization and insight was so powerful, she committed herself fully to meeting the needs of others, even though her own needs were not being met.

Although Sindhutai is undoubtedly an exceptional human being, her story also brings to light important cultural differences between the East and the West in how we see our place in the world. In Vedic sciences, we are taught from a very early age that it is through service to humanity that one becomes closer to the creator. The Hare Krishna Temple where a large part of my Vedic learning took place stresses the importance of service to man as the route to liberation. This spiritual tradition teaches us that we are part of the whole; and if I am a part of the whole, so is every other person. If you are a part of something, you have a responsibility towards it. In India, like in many places in the East, the sense of community is strong. Beyond spirituality, our sense of belonging is also a key factor that drives our responsibility.

In other words, in much of the East, *sewa* is such an integral part of our culture. Maslow, by contrast, comes from a Western, far more individualistic perspective. Some have criticized the supposed universality of his Hierarchy of Needs, arguing that his insights, while valuable, are filtered through a highly individualistic Western lens. Sindhutai's story seems to indicate that there is no universal path to self-actualization.

Although Maslow probably didn't intend his hierarchy to be interpreted this way, it can be read to imply that one cannot and should not aspire to a higher, more selfless state until one has achieved a certain level of individual achievement and comfort. In the West, and in many places influenced by the West, it is almost as if there is a checklist of personal needs that must be achieved before self-actualization and transcendence are viable possibilities. You work towards achieving your dream home, car, job, education, and family. With this comes an elevated sense of self-worth and confidence. Only when these are in place, you are prepared to start thinking about self-actualization (becoming a better version of yourself) and self-transcendence (serving humanity).

A problem arises when people focus blindly on checking off these boxes. Many get burned out in the process, and even the few who reach a pinnacle of personal achievement lack the fulfillment and joy they assumed would accompany their success. Big homes, billion-dollar companies, fancy cars, private jets. These are all signs of achievement, but without fulfillment, you will only feel hollow inside.

Achievement is in our mind. Fulfillment is in our soul. How can we even begin to compare the joy from the mind only with the happiness that radiates from the soul? In the last few years, celebrities like Robin Williams, Anthony Bourdain, Kurt Cobain, Kate Spade, and others, wildly successful by most measures, sadly took their own lives. They have taught us all an important lesson. **Achievement without fulfillment is a lonely place.**

In 'Self-love' I walked you through a thought exercise to help you define your core values. These fundamental beliefs guide you in your relationships, both personally and at work. Mindfully aligning yourself with these values is what gives you a sense of fulfillment in life. Fulfillment goes beyond achievement in that it encompasses how you go about achieving your goals, and the values by which you do so.

Interestingly, in his later years, Maslow began to question how he had placed self-actualization at the top of his pyramid of needs. He worried that this state was oriented to one's individual self, and that an even higher, other-focused state – self-transcendence – should be our ultimate aspiration.

There seems to be a growing recognition in many societies that we cannot realize our Higher Self without serving something beyond ourselves – in other words, that true self-actualization must also encompass self-transcendence. As Viktor Frankl puts it:

> *Only to the extent that someone is living out this self-transcendence of human existence, is he truly human or does he become his true self. He becomes so, not by concerning himself with his self-actualization, but by*

forgetting himself and giving himself, overlooking himself and focusing outward.

We see signs of this awareness in the desire of many millennials to work for companies that are socially responsible and give back to society. They want to work for a purpose, not just a paycheck. As the Vedic sciences have taught us for millions of years, **it is only when you move from self-centredness to selflessness that you begin to experience soul satisfaction.**

The Process of Self-realization

In the chapter on environments, 'Engineering Your Environment', we distinguished between the internal environment and the external environment. The external environment is everything you can touch, smell, see, taste, and hear. This environment is inextricably linked to the first four levels of Maslow's hierarchy (physiological needs, safety, love and belonging, self-esteem). The fifth stage (self-actualization) is all about the internal environment. When you become self-actualized, it is your perception, mindset, and thought process that change. The external environment is not necessarily altered, only your perception of it.

The Pathway from Self-actualization to Self-transcendence

We have seen the profound epiphany that put Sindhutai on a new path. I shared with you a moment in my own life when I feared I would give in to toxic feelings of resentment if I did not recover spiritually, a realization that prompted me to pause my professional life and devote time to my personal growth through monkhood.

For many of us, there comes a moment in life that forces us to pause. It could be the loss of a loved one, your age, an overwhelming sense of loneliness, or some conflict that has consumed you. This incident forces you to step back and contemplate your life. You now take stock of everything that you have. Your wealth, your family, your business, your home, your car, the quality of your life. Perhaps you see through new eyes what you have sacrificed to achieve these.

As a result of this new introspection, you become mindful of how you feel, and also of the quality of your relationships. You examine what feeds your soul, and what does not. This process draws you in. You prefer solitude and may often get lost deep in thoughts.

You now start to notice the lack of joy, contentment, happiness, fulfillment, bliss, peace, maybe even love, in your life. You start to question if the sacrifices you made were worthwhile. Do you have a sense of balance in your life? How does what you feel internally balance with what you have earned externally?

Self-actualization inevitably pushes us out of a narrow, individualistic vision of ourselves. The lines between ourselves and the world (and even the universe) start to blur. You begin to see how everything is connected. It is here that you start to notice the inequality around you. You may wonder what you have done right to receive all that you have. Thousands of people struggle and work hard, perhaps harder than you did; yet success seems to elude them. Is it fair that someone can't afford their next plate of food or good medical care?

You take notice of this. You absorb it. In all of this, a realization is born.

For the first time, you realize that the inequality in the world has nothing to do with the amount of work one puts in. You realize that you are truly blessed to receive everything that you have. And while you may have worked hard for it, the factors that have contributed to your success are too innumerable to quantify, and most of them were beyond your control.

It is at this point that gratitude is truly born. You start to appreciate everything that you have. You see your world with new rose-tinted lenses. This new appreciation shifts something inside of you. This is beyond gratitude. It is a type of pain. Not an emotional or physical pain tied to you as an individual. It is a pain that is born from what you see. When you see inequality through the eyes of gratitude, it leads to empathy. The pain you feel is empathy. You feel the plight of others around you and you can no longer care only about yourself. How can you enjoy what you have when those around you are suffering?

You now have a second wind of sorts. Another monumental shift occurs. One that results in an overwhelming feeling of abundance, and from that well of abundance, compassion is born. A compassion that is so powerful you no longer wish to be a witness to the plight of others. You now want to take action.

Compassion that inspires action now drives you. It becomes your purpose. You wake up each morning thinking how you could distance one more person from the plight they face on a daily basis.

When your daily action is born from a mindset that is geared towards eradicating the pain of someone less fortunate than you, you have achieved self-transcendence.

The Tri-factor to Transcendence

There is a phenomenal amount of research into the science of self-transcendence. Viktor Frankl, Abraham Maslow, Pamela Reed, Robert Cloninger, and Lars Tornstam have all made significant contributions to my own understanding. After examining what modern psychology has brought to the field, I found that adding a spiritual lens has further clarified my own ideas.

I've broken the process of self-transcendence into three components: two that contribute to self-actualization and a third the leads to self-transcendence.

Leading to Self-actualization:

1. **Gratitude:** When you notice the inequality in the world, the feeling within you that allows you to appreciate everything that you have.
2. **Empathy:** The pain you feel for everyone less fortunate than you.

Leading to Self-transcendence:

3. **Compassion:** The emotion that inspires you to help improve the plight of those around you.

These aren't textbook definitions, but my intention here is to present a vision of self-actualization that naturally evolves into self-transcendence. Technically, someone who is self-actualized is focused on reaching their fullest potential as an individual; they haven't necessarily incorporated that third component compelling them to contribute to the betterment of others. My tri-factor model focuses on how we can move organically from self-actualization to self-transcendence. In this vision, *'Self-actualization'*, as Viktor Frankl wonderfully observes, *'inspires us to forget ourselves, to give selflessly of ourselves, to look outward.'*

Attaining that kind of self-actualization rests entirely on the cultivation of one's internal environment. Contrary to what Maslow seems to imply, certain external conditions are not prerequisites to being inspired to serve. As we saw with Sindhutai, and in my own personal example, it was not the external environment, or a minimum level of comfort, that persuaded us to take the paths we chose.

Gratitude for what you have and empathy for others are by-products of the internal environment. We can cultivate this feeling at any stage of our life, and when we do we put ourselves in a position to serve humanity.

Redefining Success

In Maslow's model, a certain degree of individual achievement is a prerequisite for self-actualization and service. Success comes first and then you graduate to thinking about others. Alternatively, the Vedic tradition teaches us to integrate the idea of service into the fabric of our lives from early childhood. Sewa, service, self-transcendence, whatever you want to call it: we see ourselves as a part of the whole.

Let me ask you a question. **Can you name a company that has been around for more than one hundred years?** Make a list of three companies and then Google them. There is a good chance none of them is that old.

To build something that is 100 years old requires a foundation strong enough to establish a legacy. To build a legacy brand, the company will likely change management at least six times over the course of its existence. What could you do to ensure that a company survives leaderships, transitions and volatile markets over an extended period?

This may not be a perfect answer, but let's look at the case of the Tata Group in India.

India's largest employer, it has more than 100 operating companies in seven business sectors. The company has operations in more than 100 countries across six continents. This conglomerate generates more than $100 billion annually in revenue. Two thirds of the parent company, Tata Sons Ltd, is owned by philanthropic trusts that serve social and community causes for underprivileged people. Founder Jamsetji Nusserwanji says, **'The community is not just another stakeholder in business but is in fact the very purpose of our existence.'**

Would the Tata Group have survived over a hundred years if service was not at the core of its business? It is hard to say for sure, but the founders of the company attribute their success to putting philanthropy at the centre of everything they do.

In the business world, we are seeing more of this philosophy take root in other prominent companies. Brands like Toms, Nespresso, Starbucks, Lego, Spotify and more are starting to join the roster of conscious capitalism.

The world needs more people, companies, and societies that integrate service into everything they do.

Micro Giving is for Everyone

I have been fortunate enough to work with some truly accomplished individuals. If I had a cent for every time one of them told me that they want to make millions of dollars and then donate it to charity, I would probably have enough to feed a small country. While I love the idea of giving back, especially in such a magnanimous form, here is a piece of advice I generally offer.

To truly give selflessly, you have to detach yourself from the donation (it is called **dana** in Sanskrit): physically (by being known for what you have given) and mentally (holding onto the thought that you have given something). As long as the mind is still attached to its dana, it isn't selfless. It can be a means to satisfy the ego.

So, **how do you break away from being mentally attached to your selfless service?**

When I taught you how to design your environment in 'Engineering Your Environment', I encouraged you to break down your goals into macro, meso and micro goals. The micro goals are critical because they help cultivate new habits. These are the habits that allow you to achieve your bigger meso and macro goals.

When you first try to form a new habit, you are happy and proud of your ability to stick to the new habit each day, but in a few days or perhaps a fortnight, you no longer give too much thought to it. The smaller the task, the less importance you give it, even though you are executing it and enjoying the benefits it brings.

If you are walking down the street and you see a beggar on the sidewalk, let's say you gave him $1000 and walked away. A little further down the road, you met another beggar, who you gave only $10. Which of these two acts of kindness do you think you will remember for longer?

In fact, in your life, you probably cannot count the micro acts of kindness that you may have done. But you sure can remember each and every act of kindness that you deemed significant.

The secret to acting selflessly is to incorporate micro acts of kindness into your every day. The smaller the act of kindness, the less likely you are to hold on to the memory of it. I am in no way asking you to restrict your generosity, but I have seen that if you fill your day with tiny acts of kindness, you are less likely to hold on to those thoughts. This is the secret to cultivating selfless service.

Surrendering to Purpose

Let me share the story of how I became an ultra-marathon runner.

In 2002, I was working as the High Performance Coach to a professional cricket team in Kimberley, South Africa. At the start of the season, I would spend a lot of my time just sitting around watching cricket.

One afternoon one of my senior fast bowlers accused

me of laziness. Moreover, he refused to listen to any of my advice, because 'what I said was not in alignment with how I acted.' In other words, I wasn't walking the talk. That was a serious blow to my ego, but I took it on the chin and decided to do something about it.

I made a promise to the team. For every competitive day of cricket they played, I would run fifty laps around the cricket field. One lap is roughly 500 metre in circumference. That may not sound like a lot, but for someone who had not run more than 2-3 kilometres in a day, taking on the challenge of running 25 kilometres every day was quite daunting.

In the beginning it was gruelling. I was exhausted at night, sore, tending to blisters and other injuries. If you have spent any time with a professional athlete, you would understand that no amount of pain is an excuse to stop. We are just built that way.

After a month of running, I decided to run for a cause. I requested the public to donate ZAR 50 for every lap I ran to a local cancer hospice. Doing this didn't make running any easier or less painful, but I found a little more courage and resolve on the tough days.

Within two months, the cause really picked up and soon all my teammates started to join me on the runs. The boys started getting fitter and the results showed. We were cleaning up some of the country's best teams, and that year we lost in the final, an accomplishment in itself.

I ran more than 2000 kilometres that year and raised thousands of dollars for a cancer hospice.

Would I have completed this if there wasn't a cause bigger than myself? Highly unlikely.

That cricketing season changed my life. It taught me that if you are worth your salt, you will earn someone's respect and play by their rules. Athletes respect what you do more than what you say, especially if you work in performance. I would not have learned this valuable lesson if self-transcendence hadn't pushed me out of my comfort zone.

This is the thing about aligning the best version of yourself to a cause bigger than you. You learn that your well of courage and strength runs deeper than you imagined. You achieve the best version of yourself (self-actualization) because you strive for a greater cause.

Self-transcendence will push you to redefine your limits. Some of the greatest souls who have walked this earth, people I consider my heroes, have pushed their boundaries and that is why we are where we are today. Nelson Mandela, Steve Biko, Martin Luther King, Malcom X, Gandhi, Desmond Tutu, Mother Teresa, Malala Yousafzai, and so many more.

I grew up in an environment where keeping quiet was the price I had to pay to fit in. Eventually I realized fitting in wasn't even an option. But thanks to our heroes we know what freedom feels like. I often wonder what their lives must have been like.

I don't think there was a day in their lives when they weren't scared. Somehow, they found the courage to face their fears. **When you commit to self-transcendence, when you surrender to your purpose, you find a power that forges you into the person you need to be to succeed.** I have seen people in the name of a cause achieve feats beyond any imaginable comprehension. This is the power of self-transcendence.

We have reached a difficult stage in humanity. There is global political unrest, unimaginable environmental pollution, emotional and physical abuse at every level, an ongoing pandemic, discrimination, gross unemployment, and so much more. **The world needs hope and heroes now more than ever.** There is no better time to find a cause you believe in and let that cause mould you into the person you were meant to be.

Reflect back on your Ikigai-model. What are the skills that you have that can contribute to making this world a better place? And keep Moai and the power of shared purpose in mind as well. If there is one thing I know, there is more than enough love still left in your heart. I humbly request you. Channel your energy wisely.

If you want to find your purpose:

1. Answer the four Ikigai questions
2. Understand the importance of the Internal Environment
3. Familiarize yourself with the Process of Self-realization
4. Absorb the tri-factor to transcendence
5. Create your own micro-giving plan
6. Commit to it for 100 days
7. Find a community or group with whom you can experience shared purpose

Epilogue

I have a ritual. Every three months, I perform a five-day water fast. In addition to abstaining from food, I also abstain from all digital devices, social interactions, and work. It's a full detox to cleanse body and mind. I let go of the need to think, feel, speak, and act. All I do is connect with the present and observe my surroundings in a non-judgmental way. I confine myself to my home, and through mindfulness, I journey to the depths of my consciousness.

During one of these rituals, while tidying my home after my morning mindfulness practice, I noticed a tiny spider-web in the corner of my living room. A spider had woven a web that spanned a bamboo plant and a book shelf. Because I was feeling so grounded and clear, I refrained from disturbing my new friend. In fact, I was curious to observe him in his space. Every few hours, I would walk up to the web to see what he was doing. When I felt hungry, my awareness was immediately drawn to the spider. I thought, if I was feeling hungry, surely he was as well.

On the fourth morning, in a glass I had left on my dining room table, I noticed a tiny little bug. I observed it as it moved around in the glass, but at no point did it seem to me that it was trapped. After my morning meditation, I went back to the glass and noticed that the insect was still there. I thought to myself, 'Perhaps it needs a little help', so I dropped the glass on its side to allow my little winged buddy to escape.

A few moments later, it disappeared from the glass.

I recall pondering to myself, 'Am I like that little insect, trapped inside a situation I cannot recognize? Do I need someone bigger than me to help me escape as well?' In that moment of awareness, I closed my eyes and offered a prayer to the universe.

'If I am stuck, and need some guidance, please send someone to help me.'

I went about my day as normal, observing every thought and feeling in my body. This is my practice during the cleansing ritual. Enjoy the solitude and become mindful of every sensation.

The next morning was my last day of the ritual. I woke up and prepared for my meditation practice. Before sitting down, my mind was drawn to my little spider friend. I decided to go check on him before resuming my practice. There on the spider web was the tiny little winged insect. Of all the places he could have flown, he was drawn to the web. I was heartbroken as I watched him caught in the tiny claws of the spider.

During meditation, my mind kept returning to the spider. 'What was it that I needed to learn from this little drama?' I kept asking myself.

Then in meditation, a thought entered my mind. 'Did I ask the universe for the wrong guidance?' What would this experience look like through the lens of the spider? Instead of wanting to be rescued from a situation, should I have simply asked for the strength to trust that the universe will guide me, and the patience to wait for that guidance?

At times, in our quest for growth and success, we become so impatient. Perhaps, in everything, a little patience is all that is needed. Perhaps all is revealed with time. As you bring to a close your self-reflective journey within the pages of this book, let this story be a reminder that preparation (the spider building a web), patience, and trust are all essential to your growth. And a reminder, as well, of the principle with which we began this book: the impermanence of all things.

This book has been two decades in the making. It has taken me this long to commit to penning down my thoughts because it has taken me this long to ground my understanding of the concept of balance. Here is a disclosure: On one hand, I feel like my understanding of life and the pursuit of balance has come full circle. On the other hand, I feel like I have not even begun to understand it.

Amidst all this confusion, a realization emerges. If an athlete was to hold off competing until they felt perfectly in control of the necessary knowledge and experience, and of their mental and physical states, they probably would never compete. We prepare as adequately as we can, and then we trust our process and accept the outcome. Similarly, part of an artist's journey is to find the courage to leave their mark on the world and then accept whatever reverence and criticism it brings.

Twenty years later, I found the courage to leave my mark. **This book is my first stroke on the canvas of personal growth.**

On Balance

My pursuit of balance started with a question that was puzzling me. I was intrigued by the number of people searching for work-life balance or a balanced life. If you aren't one of these people, I am pretty sure you know one. What exactly is balance? What does it look like? Why do we even want balance? The more questions I asked, the fewer answers I got.

The scientist in me always believed in 'questioning the answers'. But what happens if there aren't any clear answers to the question?

An iconic representation of balance is the ancient Chinese symbol of yin and yang. Although the design is perfectly symmetrical, the underlying concept is more about dualism: the idea that opposing, contrasting forces can complement each other. It is the presence of black that allows you to recognize white, and vice versa. It is through sadness that we learn to recognize happiness. Through pain we recognize comfort. Through poverty we recognize luxury. **Without an appreciation for dualism, balance is but a figment of our imagination.**

Also, in the eastern tradition, the Buddha has well recognized a certain dualism in life and in the human predicament. He saw that, in our search for happiness and fulfillment, humans often seem to be torn between two extremes: self-denial (trying to rise above the materialism of the world) or self-indulgence (giving in to the materialism of the world). To resolve this dilemma, he taught what he called the Middle Way, described here by Jack Kornfield as:

Buddhist teaching is neither a path of denial nor of affirmation. It shows us the paradox of the universe, within and beyond the opposites. It teaches us to be in the world but not of the world. The middle way describes the middle ground between attachment and aversion, between being and non-being, between form and emptiness, between free-will and determinism. The more we delve into the middle way the more deeply we come to rest between the play of opposites.

Earlier in the book I talked about another dualism, the tension between being both actor and audience in the drama of our lives. I wrote how, by being mindfully aware of these two lenses, we can learn to become a 'witness' of our lives and the world around us: compassionate, calm, and nonjudgmental. This is what the Buddhist monk Ajahn Chah seems to be beautifully describing when he talks about the Middle Way:

Try to be mindful, and let things take their natural course. Then your mind will become still in any surroundings, like a clear forest pool. All kinds of wonderful, rare animals will come to drink at the pool, and you will clearly see the nature of all things. You will see many strange and wonderful things come and go, but you will be still. This is the happiness of the Buddha.

Writing this book has helped me become acutely aware of the dualisms in my own life and journey. On the one hand, the nature of my work with elite athletes requires me to constantly be working at the edge of their comfort zones, and my own. This fascination with extremes is not just a professional requirement, but an innate tendency. When I took up running in a serious way, I didn't just run marathons – I ran ultra-marathons. When I decided to pursue meditation, I didn't just sign up for a meditation class – I put my professional life on hold and became a monk.

I remain fascinated with extremes, and believe it is at the edge that we often experience the most growth. But I have also learnt to appreciate the value of the middle path, and of moderation. We cannot exist on the edge in all areas of our life. As I wrote about in the 'Introduction', we can only push ourselves in one domain when we have a home base or anchor in another. The relative balance or equilibrium between the four domains (Body, Mind, Relationships, Environment) will vary from person to person, and will also change and evolve over our lifetimes. But we must have stability in at least one domain. That becomes our fulcrum. For me, ever since my time in the monastery, it is my spiritual practice that is my home base. That anchor frees me up to explore and experiment in other areas. For you it will be different.

So this has become my own personal middle path: negotiating a balance between pushing myself and exploring at the edge of experience in some areas, while at the same time appreciating a middle path in other areas. I have learnt that there is balance to be found in both – the dynamic balance of the edge, and the calm, still, resting balance of the middle.

I have also learnt that an appreciation of the Middle path is essential in keeping ourselves humble. **It is at the**

extremes of experience and identity that we are most vulnerable to the trappings of ego. At one end, at the extreme of extraordinary performance and achievement, we might think of ourselves as exemplary. At the other end, in extremes of disappointment and suffering, we might feel ourselves to be shunned and excluded. In the middle, we are one with the rest of humanity – no better, no worse. In that middle, our ego and self-importance melts away.

Why is this important? **When the ego melts away, our true journey of self-discovery can begin.** We lose ourselves, only to find ourselves in a deeper way.

Without the constraints of ego, we can learn to be mindful of balance in all its forms and guises and permutations. We can find patience and humility – but also a fearless embrace of change and of the struggles and hardships that make us who we are.

In this passage, Pema Chodron wonderfully captures how all these elements come together when we walk a certain spiritual path:

> *To be fully alive, fully human, and completely awake is to be continually thrown out of the nest. To live fully alive is to be always in no-man's-land, to experience each moment as completely new and fresh. To live is to be willing to die over and over again.*

I Leave with You a Part of Me

In the introduction to this book, I highlighted the importance of the fulcrum in attempting to balance anything. In twenty years of working with professional athletes, corporate leaders, patients and children, I have seen that success and fulfillment are not the by-product of a single variable. They require the coming together of multiple factors in four key domains: Body, Mind, Relationships, and Environment. These four domains must be tightly woven, for each to impact the other. Together they constitute the ecosystem of your life. Like any ecosystem, it exists in an ever-evolving, dynamic equilibrium.

Balancing these domains in our life is no different from balancing anything else. The integrity of the fulcrum is all important. You are the fulcrum in your life, and hopefully, through the pages of this book, you learnt how to define your integrity; how to find your anchor; how to cultivate your home base.

The deeper your understanding of the self, the higher your probability of finding balance.

This is why you are the co-creator of your own destiny.

Balance for me is more than a philosophy. It has become an embodiment of everything I strive for. For those who know me, balance is probably the last word they would associate me with. Working at the cutting edge of professional sport, our lives are defined by how much time we spend outside our comfort zone. That is my life. Making the uncomfortable comfortable. In this space, it sometimes seems as if there is very little balance. Still, the peace, tranquility, bliss, harmony, and serenity I find in the middle, in my own version of the Middle Way, is something I am always cognizant of and searching for.

When I spent those years living in the temple, somewhere in my heart I found my God (Krsna). When you find your own home base, you can live your life to the fullest and without fear. When you find what anchors you, all doubt and fear will evaporate. **When you find what anchors you, the courage to challenge your comfort zone is heightened, because your point of balance is always clearly in sight.**

This book was meant to show you my pathway to balance. Like any journey, it remains a work-in-progress.

We currently live in a precarious era. Unstable political environments, climate change, discrimination, inequality, religious conflicts, and so much more. These and other pressing issues require our care and our undivided attention. Over and above these issues looms a larger problem. Our era is defined by overarching attitudes of selfishness, unequivocal greed, lack of empathy, and gross apathy. The solution to this larger problem lies in the cultivation of one's inner self. **Healing ourselves is no more optional. It is mandatory, if we are to have any hope of healing the world, with non-violence and compassion.** With folded palms, I offer my sincere prayers that my words might help in your personal journey of healing, and in our shared human journey.

I have included some validated research, many anecdotes from my patients and athletes, lessons from mentors, and teachings from a few books that have shaped my life. Above all, **I leave with you a part of my soul.** Each of my exercise was born from a place of pain, at a time when I needed clarity and courage more than ever. I pass them on to you because they have helped me, and I know in my heart they will help you.

I thank you for being a part of my journey. We are now connected, and this bond will never die.

Keep this book close to you. Read it once a year and reflect on your growth. It will be a trusted guide. Of this I am 100 per cent certain.

List of Realizations

Realization #1
You cannot heal that which you do not understand.

Realization #2
You cannot fix that which you are not prepared to change.

Realization #3
You cannot love yourself if you hate the experiences that have made you the person you are.

Realization #4
Everything you attract in your life is based on your own vibrational energy.

Realization #5
You have to see yourself as a co-creator of your destiny.

Realization #6
Your willingness to change what is working could become your greatest strength.

Realization #7
To change your current reality, you have to make the unfamiliar familiar.

Realization #8
You cannot heal yourself in the same environment that caused you pain.

Realization #9
You cannot evolve if you fear the process of growth.

Acknowledgements

When I decided to write a memoir on balance and healing, there were two things I did not expect:

1. It would present me with an opportunity to relive every incident of my life – the painful and the pleasurable.
2. With each incident came the opportunity to reflect on those who guided me every step of the way.

Writing this book was a healing journey in itself. For this opportunity, I am eternally grateful to the Pan Macmillan India team who took a chance with my ideas and supported me through it all. I am grateful to all: Rajdeep Mukherjee, Bharti Taneja, Vijay Sharma and Ditsha Gupta.

A special shout out to Avneet Kaur – my publisher who understood the importance of balancing emotions with scientific research.

None of this would have been possible without my editor, Scott Doyle. His unwavering dedication to writing mastery shines through in the way he shapes and hones a narrative. His attention to detail and remarkable editing skills have made this book what it is.

My spiritual masters and mentors: H. H. Bhakti Charu Swami, H. H. Radhanath Swami, Gauranga Das, Gaur Gopal Das and the late Shri Nealchand Vallabhjee and Shyamlal Das. It has been more than a decade since I have left the ashram, but thanks to their loving guidance in my spiritual journey, I feel blessed and nourished every single day.

All writers are attached to their words, which is why we need confidants whose advice, knowledge and inputs can guide us. Eve Lemesle and Abhishek Gupta for tirelessly reading my manuscript and challenging the 'elephants in the room'. So blessed to have you in my life.

The Life-plugin and Life-circles family whose pursuit in personal mastery is a labour of love. Gautam Khetrapal, Celia Hamitouche, Siddharth Anantharam, Seerat Bhatt, Vadim Fink, and Ronan Diego de Oliveira, thank you for pushing me outside my comfort zone.

My team: Samir Bangara, Sagar Gokhale, Anand Nanivadekar, Dolly Rateshwar, Pooja Pradaan, Ankit Agarwal, Daniel D'Silva, Jibran Khan, Kailash Gandhi, Viren Arya, Jagdish Lobo, Sushant Yattam, Pranav Singh, Juhi Mehta, Khushi Govil, Namaah Kumar (for kindly recreating the illustrations in this book), Harsh Songra, Dhaval Mevcha, Mohil Jain, Sanil Nair, Jaspreet Singh, Amit Jha, Sanjeev Asokan, Sanaa Surva, Mahendra Patel, and Lakshmi Gadkari. Your love, support and guidance is what encourages me to push the boundaries.

My family in a foreign land: Amit Mookim, Sandeep Chaudhary, Samyak Chakrabarty, Rajesh Shetty, Sheetal Sudhir, Dirga Nanjapa, Shunali Shroff (who also played a matchmaker with Pan Macmillan India), Mahesh Bhupathi, Lara Dutta, Clarabelle Saldhana, and Clestin Saldhana. Your love and encouragement gives me strength everyday.

To my patients, athletes, teams, clients, and colleagues. Thank you for trusting me through the good times and bad. Special thanks to my patients who granted me permission to use their narratives (names have been changed) and my athletes and friends who read my manuscript and provided me with quotes (Soha Ali Khan, Shunali Shroff, Mahesh Bhupati, Lara Dutta, Gaur Gopal Das, Max Mirnyi, Sania Mirza, Kristina Mänd-Lakhiani, Amit Mookim, and Brad Hodge).

To Trisha Sarang: I loved the experience of being in front of the lens for you. You are simply awesome! Thank you for this photograph on the cover.

To the scientists, researchers, doctors and academics whose works are featured in this book. Your thirst for knowledge is what moves the needles forward. With deep admiration and respect, I salute you.

To my parents, Aroon and Joystna Vallabhjee, as well as my brothers, Bhavish and Kamal Vallabhjee, for your love and support.

And lastly, thank you, to you the reader, for choosing to heal through my words.

Notes

Introduction

1. 'Story, as it turns out, was crucial to our evolution – more so than opposable thumbs. Opposable thumbs let us hang on; story told us what to hang on to. Story is what enabled us to imagine what might happen in the future, and so prepare for it – a feat no other species can claim to, opposable thumbs or not.' (Taken from Lisa Cron, *Wired for Story*)
2. An insight introduced by Daniel Kahneman in his book *Thinking, Fast and Slow*. Although a psychologist, he won the Nobel Prize in Economics because his work revolutionized our understanding of decision-making in economics and elsewhere.
3. Emotional intelligence is the quality of being aware of our own thoughts and emotions, as well as the emotions of others – and then mindfully using that awareness in how we relate to others, and to ourselves. Daniel Goleman in particular has championed the value of emotional intelligence.
4. As Goleman points out, mindfulness and emotional intelligence include not just self-awareness, but social and situational awareness.
5. Many of the 'performance hacks' I use with athletes and preview on my Instagram account (@Shayamal) where I, feature *asymmetrical training* techniques – for example, lifting with different as opposed to equal weights on either side. Such training requires intense, mindful concentration, and a very

strong engagement of core muscles. It acknowledges the fact that many of our activities in real life (such as carrying a bag of groceries) or in sport (playing tennis) are asymmetrical. More often than not, we are challenged to find stability in imbalanced situations.

6. Most of our major muscle groups appear in pairs that work in opposition to one another. For example, when our quadriceps contract, our hamstrings relax, and vice-versa. Interestingly, the optimal proportionate strength between them is not 50/50, but about 60/40. Once again, we see balance in asymmetry.

Chapter 1: Self-love

1. Peter Farley, 'A theory abandoned but still compelling,' Yale School of Medicine - https://medicine.yale.edu/news/yale-medicine-magazine/a-theory-abandoned-but-still-compelling/
2. Bessel van der Kolk, *The Body Keeps the Score: Brain, Mind, and Body in the Healing of Trauma*

Chapter 2: Circles of Connection

1. Also known as 'the Dunbar number,' usually rounded off at 150. This is misleading, in that it represents the maximum number of people with whom we can maintain 'stable' social relations. In fact, Dunbar proposed a series of nested, concentric numbers – much like my own, but with more layers. The best summary of his research can be found in the *New Yorker* article I've listed in the references.

Chapter 3: Start with Your Strengths

1. The Sigmoid Curve actually began as a mathematical model used to explain population growth. Charles Handy, a writer who focused on organizational behavior, applied the basic principle

to how successful organizations and individuals can continually grow and evolve.

2. You can take the test at https://www.gallup.com/cliftonstrengths/en/home.aspx

Chapter 4: Playing with Perspective

1. Neuroplasticity refers to the brain's ability to change, evolve, and adapt throughout one's lifetime, and not just in one's formative years. A big breakthrough in the field came when doctors observed how stroke victims, despite severe damage to parts of their brains, could eventually regain lost functions. Healthy regions of the brain learned to take over temporarily impaired functions.
2. This is related to what psychologists call our *locus of control*—in other words, what is the location, the pivot, the fulcrum, of the forces shaping our lives. If that locus is internal, we say to ourselves, 'I control my own destiny.' If that locus is external, we think, 'Others, or fate, control my destiny.' A major tenet of positive psychology is that we can, over time, cultivate an internal locus of control—and that doing so contributes significantly to our happiness and success.
3. Another way of looking at these two lenses comes from Martin Seligman, the founder of Positive Psychology. Seligman wrote about the concepts of *learned helplessness,* on the one hand, and *learned optimism* on the other. As these terms imply, while some people are innately more optimistic or pessimistic, these attitudes are fluid, or plastic. They can be learned and unlearned.

Chapter 6: Engineering Your Environment

1. These terms come from an approach to elite athletic training called Periodization in which your training is broken down into macrocycles, mesocycles, and microcycles.

Bibliography

A., Van der Kolk Bessel. *The Body Keeps the Score: Brain, Mind, and Body in the Healing of Trauma*. NY, NY: Penguin Books, 2015.

Abdelhamid, Tariq Sami. 'The Self-Destruction and Renewal of Lean Construction Theory: A Prediction From Boyd's Theory'. *Semantic Scholar*, January 1, 1970. https://bit.ly/2vBDyqW

Abraham Maslow: *The Hierarchy of Needs*. Corby: Institute of Management Foundation, 1998.

Ackerman, Courtney E. 'What Is Neuroplasticity? A Psychologist Explains [+14 Exercises].' *PositivePsychology*, October 9, 2019. https://bit.ly/3desC3e.

Anima Sound Medicine. 'Solfeggio Frequencies - The Healing Tones of Creation.' *Anima Sound Medicine*. Accessed March 14, 2020. https://bit.ly/2TZ2K3QBaker

Anita Satyajit. 'Sindhutai Sapkal Was Begging at Train Stations When She Found Her Calling – Helping Street Children.' *The Christian Science Monitor*, December 10, 2015. https://bit.ly/2Ugvcx6.

Atzil, Shir, Talma Hendler, and Ruth Feldman. 'The Brain Basis of Social Synchrony.' *Social Cognitive and Affective Neuroscience*. Oxford University Press, August 2014. https://bit.ly/390Axy6.

Behary, Wendy T. *Disarming the Narcissist: Surviving & Thriving with the Self-Absorbed*. Oakland, CA: New Harbinger Publications, Inc., 2013.

Bennett-Goleman, Tara. *Emotional Alchemy: How Your Mind Can Heal Your Heart*. London: Rider, 2001.

Benson, Herbert, Eileen M. Stuart, and Michael P. Goldberg. *The Wellness Book: The Comprehensive Guide to Maintaining Health and Treating Stress-Related Illness*. New York: Scribner, 2010.

Bhattacharjee, Samita. 'A Value-Driven Organization: Tata from the Perspective of an Insider.' Essay. In *Another State of Mind*, n.d.

Blachowicz, Maralyn Kay. *Abraham Maslow: The Viability of a Humanistically Grounded Value Theory*, 1971.

Bob. Jerry Seinfeld's Productivity Hack: Don't Break the Chain! *Medium,* April 29, 2019. https://bit.ly/2xbHMpm

Bostock, David. *Aristotle's Ethics*. Oxford: Oxford University Press, 2000.

Breazeale, Daniel, and R. J. Hollingdale. *Nietzsche: Untimely Meditations*. Cambridge: Cambridge University Press, 1997.

Brennan, Patrick McKinley. 'Self-Love and Forgiveness: A Holy Alliance?' SSRN, July 1, 2009. https://bit.ly/3a95kdu

Brown, Brene. *Daring Greatly: How the Courage to Be Vulnerable Transforms the Way We Live, Love, Parent, and Lead.* Penguin Random House, 2017.

Brown, Brene. *Power of Vulnerability: Teachings on Authenticity, Connection, and Courage*. Sounds True, Incorporated, 2012.

Buckingham, Marcus, and Donald O. Clifton. *Now, Discover Your Strengths: How to Develop Your Talents and Those of the People You Manage*. London: Pocket Books, 2005.

Buettner, Dan. 'How to Live to Be 100+.' TED: Ideas worth spreading, n.d. https://bit.ly/3b53f2b

Buettner, Dan. *Thrive - Finding Happiness the Blue Zones Way*. National Geographic Society, 2011.

Buffet, Mary and David Clark. *The New Buffettology: the Proven Techniques for Investing Successfully in Changing Markets That Have Made Warren Buffett the World's Most Famous Investor*. New York: Simon & Schuster, 2002.

Building the High-Performance Workforce: A Quantitative Analysis of the Effectiveness of Performance Management Strategies: Executive Briefing. Washington, D.C.: Corporate Leadership Council, 2003.

Bunch, Jim. 'The 9 Environments That Make Up Your Life with Jim Bunch.' *Unmistakable Creative*, August 23, 2018. https://bit.ly/33sx3TT /.

Carley, Steven G. *Abraham Maslow: Holistic-Dynamic Theory*. Fall River, MA: SGC Production, 2015.

Chödrön Pema. *When Things Fall Apart: Heart Advice for Difficult Times*. London: Thorsons Classics, 2017.

Christensen, Villy, and Daniel Pauly.'ECOPATH II - a Software for Balancing Steady-State Ecosystem Models and Calculating Network Characteristics.' *Semantic Scholar*, January 1, 1992. https://bit.ly/2WqHaXR

Clear, James. *Atomic Habits: An Easy and Proven Way to Build Good Habits and Break Bad Ones*. London: Cornerstone, 2019.

Cloninger, C. Robert. *Feeling Good: the Science of Well-Being*. Oxford: Oxford University Press, 2004.

Cloninger, Robert. *Personality and Psychopathology*. Washington: American Psychopathological Association, 1999.

Covey, Stephen R. *The 7 Habits of Highly Effective People*. London: Simon & Schuster, 2005.

Cromie, William J. 'Meditation Changes Temperatures: Mind Controls Body in Extreme Experiments'. *The Harvard Gazette,* April 18, 2002.

Cron, Lisa. *Wired for Story: The Writer's Guide to Using Brain Science to Hook Readers from the Very First Sentence*. New York: Ten Speed Press, 2012.

Csikszentmihalyi, Mihaly. *Flow and the Foundations of Positive Psychology*. The Collection Works of Mihaly Csikszentnihalyi. Springer, 2016.

Csikszentmihalyi, Mihaly. *Flow: the Psychology of Optimal Experience*. New York: Harper Row, 2009.

Derick, Jenson. 'The Plants Respond.' The Sun Magazine. July 1997. Accessed March 14, 2020https://bit.ly/2vyv3NlPlato, and C. J. Rowe. *Symposium: Plato*. Warminster: Aris & Phillips, 1998.

Dobson, Deborah J. G., and Keith S. Dobson. *Evidence-Based Practice of Cognitive-Behavioral Therapy*. New York: The Guildford Press, 2018.

Dobson, S. Keith. *Handbook of Cognitive-Behavioural Therapies.* London: Hutchinson, 1988.

Eells, Josh. 'Cleve Backster Talked to Plants. And They Talked Back.' *The New York Times*, December 21, 2013. https://nyti.ms/3a55xOD

Emoto, Masaru. *The Hidden Messages in Water.* New York: ATRIA Books, 2005.

Epstein, David J. *The Sports Gene: inside the Science of Extraordinary Athletic Performance.* NY, NY: Current, 2014.

Farley, Peter. 'A Theory Abandoned but Still Compelling.' *Yale Medicine Magazine.* Yale School of Medicine, September 15, 2008. https://bit.ly/2UmdZCz

Farrell, Joan M. *Experiencing Schema Therapy from the Inside Out.* Guilford Publications, 2018.

Farrell, Joan M., Neele Reiss, and Ida A. Shaw. *The Schema Therapy Clinician's Guide: a Complete Resource for Building and Delivering Individual, Group and Integrated Schema Mode Treatment Programs.* Chichester, West Sussex: John Wiley & Sons, Ltd., 2014.

Finkelstein, L. 'What Is Not Measurable, Make Measurable'. *SAGE Journals.* Accessed March 19, 2020. https://bit.ly/2WpVIH2.

Fogg, B. J. *Tiny Habits: the Small Changes That Change Everything.* Boston: Houghton Mifflin Harcourt, 2020.

Frankl, Viktor E. *Man's Search for Ultimate Meaning.* London: Rider, 2011.

Frankl, Viktor E., and Shimon Dovid. Cowen. *Viktor Frankl: Text and Commentary.* St Kilda, Vic.: Institute for Judaism and Civilization Inc., 2011.

Frankl, Viktor E., Daniel Goleman, and Franz Vesely. *Yes to Life: in Spite of Everything.* Boston: Beacon Press, 2020.

Frankl, Viktor E., Ilse Lasch, Harold S. Kushner, and William J. Wnislade. *Man's Search for Meaning.* Boston, MA: Beacon Press, 2015.

Frankl, Viktor E., Junji Nagasawa, and Yuji Takeuchi. *The Will to Meaning.* Tokyo: Bunri, 1972.

Frankl, Viktor. 1979 *The Unheard Cry for Meaning: Psychotherapy and Humanism*. New York: Simon and Schuster, n.d.

García Héctor, Francesc Miralles, and Heather Cleary. *Ikigai: the Japanese Secret to a Long and Happy Life*. Waterville, ME: Thorndike Press Large Print, 2018.

Gendun, Anila Rinchen. Palmo, and Shammar. *Working with the Emotions*. Montignac, France: Dzambala, 1992.

Geoffrey Mock. 'Synchronicity at Duke.' *Duke Today*. Accessed March 14, 2020https://bit.ly/3a39G5K.

Georgiades, Evelina, Vassilis Klissouras, Jamie Baulch, Guan Wang, and Yannis P. Pitsiladis. 'Why Nature Prevails over Nurture in the Making of the Elite Athlete: Semantic Scholar.' undefined, January 1, 1970. https://bit.ly/2U5ueoN

Goleman, D. *Emotional Intelligence: Why It Can Matter More than IQ*. Bloomsbury., n.d.

Grant, Adam. *Give and Take: a Revolutionary Approach to Success*. London: Weidenfeld & Nicolson, 2014.

Grenyer, Brin F. S. 'The Clinician's Dilemma: Core Conflictual Relationship Themes in Personality Disorders.' Australian Clinical Psychology Association, July 4, 2012. https://bit.ly/3b9pAf6

Haidt, Jonathan. *The Happiness Hypothesis: Finding Modern Truth in Ancient Wisdom*. New York: Basic Books, a member of the Perseus Books Group, 2006.

Hammond, Grant Tedrick. *The Mind of War: John Boyd and American Security*. Washington: Smithsonian Books, 2012.

Handy, Charles B. *The Age of Paradox*. Boston, MA: Harvard Business School, 1995.

Harcourt, Edward. 'Self-Love and Practical Rationality.' Morality and the Emotions. Accessed March 19, 2020. https://bit.ly/2x3yR9D.

Harrell, Eben. 'How 1% Performance Improvements Led to Olympic Gold.' *Harvard Business Review*, October 30, 2015. https://bit.ly/2Wra22c

Harvey, Arthur W. *Abraham Maslow: Implications for the Development of Creative Music Educators*. Ann Arbor, MI: Univ. Microfilms, 1979.

Holt-Lunstad, Julianne. 'So Lonely I Could Die'. American Psychological Association. Published on 5 Augurst 2017. Accessed March 14, 2020. https://bit.ly/393RW8Q

Imai, Masaaki. *Kaizen: the Key to Japan's Competitive Success*. New York: McGraw-Hill, 1991.

Jackson, Matthew O. 'The Friendship Paradox and Systematic Biases in Perceptions and Social Norms,' November 2017. https://arxiv.org/pdf/1605.04470.pdf.

James Clear. 'How to Stop Procrastinating by Using the "Seinfeld Strategy."' *James Clear*, February 4, 2020. https://bit.ly/2TZQWys

Jantz, Gregory L. *Healing the Scars of Addiction: Reclaiming Your Life and Moving into a Healthy Future*. Grand Rapids: Revell, a division of Baker-Publishing Group, 2018.

Jantz, Gregory L. 'Brain Differences Between Genders.' *Psychology Today.* Published on Feb 2014). Sussex Publishers. Accessed March 14, 2020. https://bit.ly/3dbofWS

Jensen, Derrick. 'The Plants Respond: An Interview with Cleve Backster.', *The Sun,* July 1997. Accessed on 19 March 2020. https://bit.ly/3b3QAwc

Jørgensen, Sven Erik. *Ecological Modelling: an Introduction*. Southampton: WIT Press, 2009.

Kabat-Zinn, J. 'Mindfulness Based Stress Reduction (MBSR). Constructivism in the Human Sciences.' Kabat-Zinn, J. (2003). Mindfulness Based Stress Reduction (MBSR). *Constructivism in the Human Sciences*, 8, 73-83. - References - Scientific Research Publishing. Accessed March 14, 2020. https://bit.ly/3ddE1k7

Kabat-Zinn, Jon. *Coming to Our Senses: Healing Ourselves and the World through Mindfulness.* New York: Hachette Books, 2016.

Kapleau, Philip. *The Three Pillars of Zen*. New York: Anchor Books, 1989.

Katzenbach, Jon R., and Douglas K. Smith. *The Wisdom of Teams.* London: McGraw-Hill, 1998.

Konnikova, Maria. 'The Limits of Friendship.' *The New Yorker*, June 20, 2017. https://bit.ly/3deqLLO

Kornfield, Jack, and Gil Fronsdal. *Teachings of the Buddha*. Boston, MA: Shambhala, 2012.

Kornfield, Jack. *The Wise Heart: a Guide to the Universal Teachings of Buddhist Psychology*. New York: Bantam Books, 2009.

Kotler, Steven. *The Rise of Superman: Decoding the Science of Ultimate Human Performance*. London: Quercus, 2015.

Kubler-Ross, Elisabeth, and Rosemary Ronald. *On Death and Dying*. Auckland, N.Z.: Royal New Zealand Foundation of the Blind, 2013.

Lewis, C. S. *The Four Loves*. Brantford, Ont.: W. Ross MacDonald School Resource Services Library, 2017.

Lopez, Donald S. *The Madman's Middle Way: Reflections on Reality of the Tibetan Monk Gendun Chopel*. Chicago (Ill.): The University of Chicago Press, 2006.

Luborsky, Lester, and Paul Crits-Christoph. *Understanding Transference: the Core Conflictual Relationship Theme Method*. Washington, DC: American Psychological Association, 2003.

Madsen, Kristen Bent. *Abraham Maslow*. København: Forum, 1981.

Mann, Don D. *The Modern Day Gunslinger: the Ultimate Handgun Training Manual*. New York: Skyhorse Pub., 2010.

Maslow, Abraham H. *The Power of Self-Actualization*, n.d.

Maslow, Abraham H. *Theory of Human Motivation*. S.l.: Wilder Publications, 2018.

Maslow, Abraham H., and Robert Frager. *Motivation and Personality*. New Delhi: Pearson Education, 1987.

Mihaly, Kata., 'Do More Friends Mean Better Grades?' *Rand Population Research Centre*, 2009. https://bit.ly/2UgVRKo.

Miles, Robert P. *Warren Buffett Wealth: Principles and Practical Methods Used by the World's Greatest Investor*. Hoboken: John Wiley & Sons, 2014.

Miller, Donald. *Scary Close: Dropping the Act and Finding True Intimacy*. Nashville, TN: Nelson Books, 2015.

Nelson, Shasta. *Frientimacy - How to Deepen Friendships for Lifelong Health and Happiness*. Seal Press, 2016.

Nietzsche, Friedrich Wilhelm, and Ron King. *Maxims and Arrows--Nietzche (Sic!)*. Guildford: Circle Press Publications, 1970.

Patañjali, and Alfred Scheepers. *The Yoga Sūtras of Pantañjali*. Amsterdam: Olive Press, 1997.

Patañjali, Vyāsa, Āraṇya Hariharānanda, and Paresh Nath Mukerji. *Yoga Philosophy of Patañjali: Containing His Yoga Aphorisms, with Commentary of Vyāsa in Original Sanskrit and Annotations Thereon, with Copious Hints on the Practice of Yoga*. Calcutta: University of Calcutta, 1981.

'Periodization of Training' in *Exercise and Sport Science,* edited by William E. Garrett, Jr and Donald T. Kirkendall, London: Lippincott Williams & Wilkins, 2000.

'Pranayama.' *Wikipedia*. Wikimedia Foundation, March 2, 2020. https://bit.ly/33BoTZq

Peterson, Christopher, and Martin E. P. Seligman. *Character Strengths and Virtues: a Handbook and Classification*. Oxford: Oxford University Press, 2004.

Phōthiyānathēra Phra, Jack Kornfield, and Paul Breiter. *A Still Forest Pool: the Insight Meditation of Achaan Chah*. Wheaton, IL: Quest Books, Theosophical Publishing House, 2014.

Rampenthal, Chas. 'Workplace Dating: The New Rules.' Inc.com. Inc., September 18, 2012. https://bit.ly/38VcXCM.

Reed, Pamela G. 'Practitioner as Theorist: A Reprise.' *Nursing Science Quarterly* 21.4 (2008): 315-321.

Reed, Pamela G. 'Self-Transcendence Theory.' *Nursology*, n.d. https://bit.ly/2vxlWLz.

Reed, Pamela G., and Nelma B. Crawford Shearer. *Nursing Knowledge and Theory Innovation: Advancing the Science of Practice*. New York, NY: Springer Publishing Company, LLC, 2017.

Reis, Harry, et. al. 'Familiarity Does Indeed Promote Attraction in Live Interactions.' *Journal of Personality and Social Psychology,* 101(3):557-70 · March 2011. https://bit.ly/38X9fbK.

Resnick, Brian. 'Loneliness Actually Hurts Us on a Cellular Level.' *Vox*, January 30, 2017. https://bit.ly/2UjE0lR.

Ridley, Matt. *Nature via Nurture: Genes, Experience, and What Makes Us Human*. London: Fourth Estate, 2011.

Roberts, Andrew Lawrence. *The Thinking Student's Guide to*

College: 75 Tips for Getting a Better Education. Chicago: The University of Chicago Press, 2010.

Robertson, Donald. *Stoicism and the Art of Happiness: Practical Wisdom for Everyday Life*. London: John Murray Learning, 2018.

Rousseau, Denise M. 'Schema, Promise and Mutuality: The Building Blocks of the Psychological Contract.' Wiley Online Library. John Wiley & Sons, Ltd, December 16, 2010. https://bit.ly/2UnXiqa.

S., Saraswati S. *Asana Pranayama Mudra Bandha*. Bihar: Bihar Yoga Bharati, 1996.

Schippers, Michaela. 'Team Reflexivity and Innovation.', *Journal of Management,* March 2012.

Segal, Uzi. 'The Ellsberg Paradox and Risk Aversion: An Anticipated Utility Approach.' International Economic Review. Department of Economics, University of Pennsylvania and Osaka University Institute of Social and Economic Research Association, January 1, 1987. https://bit.ly/33sO9kx.

Segall, Seth Robert. *Encountering Buddhism: Western Psychology and Buddhist Teachings*. Albany: State University of New York Press, 2003.

Seligman, Martin E. P. *Learned Optimism: How to Change Your Mind and Your Life*. London: Nicholas Brealey Publishing, 2018.

Seneca, Lucius Annaeus. *Letters from a Stoic*. United States: CreateSpace Independent Publishing Platform, 2016.

Shorter, Edward. *From the Mind into the Body: the Cultural Origins of Psychosomatic Symptoms*. New York: Free Press, 1994.

Smith, Mary Jane, and Patricia R. Liehr. *Middle Range Theory for Nursing*. New York, NY: Springer publishing company, 2018.

Stambaugh, Joan. *Impermanence Is Buddha-Nature: Dogen's Understanding of Temporality*. Honolulu, HI: University of Hawaii, 1990.

Stern, Doreen. 'Be Like Jerry Seinfeld: Create a Chain.' Society of Actuaries, March 2019. https://bit.ly/2UjejBZ

Stoerkel, Erika. 'Can Random Acts of Kindness Increase Well-Being?' PositivePsychology.com, July 4, 2019. Accessed on March 14, 2020. https://bit.ly/2Wox1dZ

Streeter, Kurt. 'The Crowd Roars for Federer, and Djokovic Tunes Out the Noise.' *The New York Times*, July 15, 2019. https://nyti.ms/3derQDm

Sussman, Robert W., and C. Robert. Cloninger. *Origins of Cooperation and Altruism*. New York: Springer, 2011.

Swami, Radhanath. 'Selfless Service: Radhanath Swami - Quotes.' Radhanath Swami Quotes. Accessed March 14, 2020. https://bit.ly/3dbIrrK.

Tara, Bennett-Goleman. *Emotional Alchemy: How Your Mind Can Heal Your Heart*. GREAT BRITAN: Rider, 2003.

Tartakovsky, Margarita. 'Cultivating an Internal Locus of Control - and Why It's Crucial.' World of Psychology, July 8, 2018. https://bit.ly/2U23Uvy.

Tartakovsky, Margarita. 'Cultivating an Internal Locus of Control - and Why It's Crucial.' *World of Psychology*, July 8, 2018. https://bit.ly/33uBXQ4.

The Bible: New King James Version. Nashville: Thomas Nelson, 2015.

The Editors of Encyclopaedia Britannica. 'Rorschach Test | Definition | Britannica.' Accessed March 14, 2020. https://bit.ly/2xaRrNi.

The Washington Post. 'Why Athletes Should Treat the Brain like a Muscle.' *The Washington Post*. WP Company, April 11, 2017. https://wapo.st/3desj8A.

'Thomas-Kilmann Conflict Mode Instrument.' *Psychometrics* Canada. Accessed March 19, 2020. https://bit.ly/2QuGEUN.

Tompkins, Peter and. Christopher Bird. *The Secret Life of Plants: A Fascinating Account of the Physical, Emotional, and Spiritual Relations Between Plants and Man*. Harper Paperbacks, 2018.

Tornstam, Lars. *Gerotranscendence: a Developmental Theory of Positive Aging*. New York: Springer, 2005.

Tutu, Desmond. *No Future Without Forgiveness*. London: Ebury Digital, 2012.

University of California - Los Angeles. 'Putting Feelings Into Words Produces Therapeutic Effects In The Brain.' *ScienceDaily*. https://bit.ly/2Wswgka

Vaillant, George E. 'Positive Emotions, Spirituality and the Practice of Psychiatry.' Mens sana monographs. Medknow Publications, January 2008. https://bit.ly/33uG8v8.

Vālmīki, Robert P. Goldman, and Sutherland Goldman Sally J. *The Ramayana of Valmiki: an Epic of Ancient India*. Princeton: Princeton University Press, 2016.

Vaughan, Mike. *The Thinking Effect: Rethinking Thinking to Create Great Leaders and the New Value Worker*. Boston: Nicholas Brealey Publishing, 2013.

Vogt, Eric E., Juanita Brown, and David Isaacs. *The Art of Powerful Questions: Catalyzing, Insight, Innovation, and Action*. Mill Valley, CA: Whole Systems Associates, 2003.

Vreeswijk, Michiel van. *Mindfulness and Schema Therapy: a Practical Guide*. Chichester, West Sussex: John Wiley & Sons, 2014.

Watts, Alan. 'The Myopic View of the World' by Alan Watts (Complete Lecture and Transcript).' The Organism.Earth Library. Accessed March 14, 2020. https://bit.ly/3a2LW1B.

Williams, Ted, John Underwood, and Robert Cupp. *The Science of Hitting*. New York, NY: Simon & Schuster, 2013.

Worthington, Everett L. *Forgiveness and Reconciliation: Theory and Applications*. London: Routledge, 2014.

Young, Jeffrey E., Janet S. Klosko, and Aaron T. Beck. *Reinventing Your Life: the Bestselling Breakthrough Program to End Negative Behaviour and Feel Great*. Brunswick, Victoria: Scribe, 2019.

Young, Jeffrey, and Janet Klosko. *Schema Therapy: a Practitioner's Guide*. New York: Guilford Publications, 2006.

'Zane Robertson Smashes New Zealand Half-Marathon Record in Japan.' *Stuff,* February 01, 2015. Accessed March 14, 2020. https://bit.ly/3a93IjW

Zeiger, Joanna. *The Champion Mindset: an Athlete's Guide to Mental Toughness*. New York: St. Martin's Griffin, 2017.